The Coming of the Mormons

In the bitter February days of 1846, the Mormon wagon train started westward from Illinois. It was the beginning of a two-thousand-mile journey across the wilderness toward Salt Lake Valley—a desert which no one else wanted. By late spring some twenty thousand people were on the way in one of the most remarkable migrations in history.

These were not adventurers seeking their fortune in the wilderness. They were earnest members of the so-called Mormon Church, seeking freedom to worship as they pleased and a peaceful locality for their way of life.

Skillfully Jim Kjelgaard has recounted the mighty migration of the Mormons. To read their story is to feel new pride in the vision and determination of these early Americans.

THE
COMING OF
THE MORMONS

by JIM KJELGAARD

Illustrated by STEPHEN J. VOORHIES

Landmark
BOOKS

RANDOM HOUSE · NEW YORK

978
Kje
9-71

cp. 1

7 868

Contents

The Coming of the Mormons

1. Trouble In Illinois

IN THE PLEASANT CITY OF NAUVOO, ILLINOIS, Joseph Smith, founder of the Church of Jesus Christ of Latter-Day Saints, or Mormons, as they are more commonly known, sat alone in his study. His gentle face was heavy with worry and his eyes were filled with unshed tears.

3

Only an hour before a courier had brought more bad news. Thomas Watley, a Mormon farmer who lived three miles from Nauvoo, lay dead in his dooryard with a bullet hole through his head. His home was in ashes. His wife and children were being brought into Nauvoo, where they hoped to find a refuge.

Joseph Smith brushed a hand across his face, and only made more clear the sorrow written there. It was not pity for himself that he felt, or concern for himself. This man, born to be a leader of other men, grieved for all who had fallen like Thomas Watley. He grieved for all the hardships that the Mormons had endured on the long, hard trail that had finally brought them to the banks of the Mississippi.

It had been a dismal, difficult journey that long ago would have broken the hearts of a people less determined and less courageous. Starting in Joseph Smith's boyhood home, the hamlet of Palmyra, New York, it had led to Kirtland, Ohio. From there the Mormons' determination to think and to worship as they saw fit had taken them to Independence, Missouri.

Finally the trail had led back to Nauvoo, and along all of it there had been no peace for the Mormons. Always they had been hated and persecuted.

It was a time of great religious activity, with the various faiths loudly disagreeing with each other. Joseph Smith's claim that he had been visited by Divine Personages was received with great scorn. More abuse was heaped upon him when he declared that he had been visited again, this time by the Angel Moroni. According to Smith, the Angel Moroni revealed to him both the hiding place of the golden plates upon which was written *The Book of Mormon* and the means for translating them. This roused believers in other faiths to mighty anger.

Joseph Smith, deep in thought, stared at the window of his study and did not even see it.

In the East, the Mormons were persecuted and despised largely because of their religious beliefs. But what they had suffered in the East was as nothing to what they met on the supposedly free American frontier.

Few Mormons had ever voluntarily harmed, or wanted to harm, anyone. Yet, the evil reputation that had attached itself to them in the East had not only followed them to the West but, like a snowball rolling downhill, had increased all out of proportion. Joseph Smith thought of the reasons for this.

The frontier was a place where almost the only law lay in the rifle a man held in his hands or the pistol at his belt. With the exception of the Mormons, a fair proportion of the people in Illinois were eagerly sought by law authorities elsewhere. Such people could, and would, do anything at all. Then, after they had robbed, pillaged, or even murdered, they said, "A Mormon did it." Because the Mormons already had a bad reputation, few people even listened to anything they said in their own defense.

The Mormons believed in industry and thrift.

They had bought the land where Nauvoo now stood when all others considered it only a malaria-infested swamp. They had drained the swamps, cut the forests, and built a city. By far the most modern and most progressive city on the frontier, Nauvoo was three times the size of struggling Chicago. Border roughnecks who were too lazy to build for themselves wanted to take, by force, what the Mormons had created by hard work.

The Mormons were still hated for their religion, which many ill-informed people considered heathenish. Certain politicians feared the massed strength of the Mormons and the collective votes they could command. Partly because the Mormons did not believe in slavery, Missouri's governor, L. W. Boggs, had given them three days to get out of Missouri. Otherwise, they would be turned over to the mob that was howling for their blood. They had been able to take with them only such goods as their ox- or mule-drawn wagons would hold.

During the fighting in Missouri, Joseph Smith himself and his brother, Hyrum, had been imprisoned. Joseph and Hyrum had been sentenced to death, but they had escaped their guards and made their way to Nauvoo.

Joseph Smith rested his strong chin in his right hand.

Beyond any doubt, the Mormons themselves were to blame for a part of their troubles. There were a certain few among them who were unable to restrain boastful tongues. The Mormons, they said, would inherit the earth. Was not that the word of their Prophet, Joseph Smith? (It mattered not to them that they had misinterpreted the word, for Joseph Smith had never believed, or taught, that the Mormons were destined to rule the earth. Furthermore, he had always taught tolerance for all people.) It could not help arousing more antagonism when a Mormon told his neighbor, who might not be a Mormon, that he would not have his farm very long because the Mormons were going to get everything.

Finally, among the Mormons there were a number of men who were as hot-headed as anyone else on the border. They would not run from or even try to avoid a fight, but were just as willing to battle their neighbors as the neighbors were to fight them. Joseph Smith himself, seeing his family in danger, would have defended them to the best of his ability and with whatever weapons were at hand.

Again the great sorrow, the all-enfolding sympathy, crept over his face. But it was still not sorrow for himself or sympathy for himself. In all his life this man, strong enough to found a completely new religion and to make it thrive in the face of increasing persecution, had never had a single thought for himself.

From the beginning he had hoped for peace for his people, not the constant war which so far had been their lot. He had sought to lead the Mormons to peace in New York, in Ohio, in Missouri, and finally, here in Illinois. Apparently peace was hard to find.

Joseph Smith set his jaw and fire glowed in his eyes. He had brought the Mormons this far and he would lead them farther. Never once was there thought of abandoning hope or of surrendering to the enemy. Joseph Smith wrapped himself a little more deeply in the blanket of thought that was about him.

"Take your people to the Rocky Mountains."

Joseph Smith sat up, and for a moment he was startled. He looked about the study. He was alone; there was no one present except himself. Had someone spoken, or had the words arisen from the depths of his own mind? He could see no one, yet he was sure that he had heard clearly.

His troubled mind was suddenly at peace. There was no more questioning, no more soul-searching. He knew, at last, what the Mormons must do and where they must go. To be sure, the Rocky Mountains, and almost everything else west of the Missouri, was a wilderness. However, by this time some 200 wagons and at least 2,000 settlers had started for the free, fertile lands of the Oregon territory.

The Great Plains and the Rocky Mountains composed the Dark Land. Even so great a man as Daniel Webster, lecturing in the halls of the United States Congress, had pronounced it waste and desert, fit only for wild beasts and savages; the less the United States had to do with it, the better off they would be. And Daniel Webster was not alone in such thoughts.

The West was vaguely known as Oregon, The Great Basin, California. It was a place where no sane man would go by himself, to say nothing of taking with him thousands of men, women, and children, as well as cattle, horses, wagons, seeds, plows, and the numerous other possessions they would need just to keep alive.

Nevertheless, Joseph Smith was happy and he no longer had any doubt. If the Mormons could not live in the United States, and experience had proven that they could not, they would leave.

Joseph Smith left his study and went to the meeting place of the twelve apostles, the twelve men who were highest in the councils of the Mormon Church. He looked fondly at the twelve. Some of them, notably Heber Kimball and Brigham Young, had been with him almost from the start. Of all the twelve, Brigham Young, who had once walked two hundred and fifty miles through mud and snow to carry Joseph Smith's word to others, was probably nearest his heart. Joseph Smith spoke to the twelve officials.

"We will find our Zion," he said, "in the Rocky Mountains."

And the twelve, who had never known this man to speak falsely to them or to anyone else, believed.

Joseph Smith was never to lead his people to their Promised Land. Never once had the Mormons successfully appealed to duly-constituted

Joseph Smith spoke earnestly to his twelve apostles.

officials for protection of either their persons or their property. In 1844 the Mormons decided that they themselves must fill some posts of authority. They would run Joseph Smith for President of the United States, and use every lawful means in their power to elect him. Some two hundred and fifty Mormon officials, including Brigham Young, went forth to campaign for their beloved leader.

While they were away, Thomas Ford, the Governor of Illinois, caused Joseph and Hyrum Smith, and other leading Mormons, to be arrested and placed in the jail at Carthage, Illinois. On June 27, 1844, a mob of ruffians stormed the jail, and Joseph and Hyrum Smith died in the hail of bullets that were shot into the structure.

2. A New Leader

WHEN THEIR LEADERS WERE MURDERED, ten of the apostles were in various parts of the East to do all they could to help elect Joseph Smith to the Presidency. There were no telephone, telegraph, radio, or even any trains that were dependable. Therefore, messages were slow.

Brigham Young and Orson Pratt, an Elder of the Mormon Church, were in the East when the terrible news reached them.

By trade Brigham Young was a carpenter and glazier. His entire formal education consisted of exactly eleven days in school. Although more schooling would have helped Brigham Young, he was by nature such a strong, forceful, and intelligent man, that lack of education could not keep him from rising to high places. Like Joseph Smith, he was a born leader.

He had allied himself with the Mormons for the same reason that any sincere person devotes his time and energies to any cause. He believed in Mormonism with his heart and soul. Already he had accomplished miracles as a Mormon missionary, making at least one trip to England, and never had he received so much as one penny for this work. Always he had depended on his own resources to support himself and to raise money for the cause he was trying to further.

His love for Joseph Smith was much more

than a brotherly love. To Brigham Young, Joseph Smith was The Prophet, a man to be adored and revered. The news of his death was shocking, and even more shocking was the way he had died. But, though Brigham Young suffered heartbreak and had time for tears, he also saw the need for action.

He did not linger in New Hampshire, but went at once to Boston where he met Wilford Woodruff, who was later to be President of the Mormon Church. From Boston word was sent to the other apostles. They were to gather in Boston, the message said, and by July 23 eight of them were there. Two of the apostles, Parley Pratt and George Smith, took a different route and arrived in Nauvoo August 3. The eight in Boston started at once for their headquarters city.

They took the train to Buffalo, where they boarded a lake steamer for Detroit. From Detroit they traveled by steamer to Chicago, and transferred to the stage for Galena, Illinois. At

Galena they took a river steamer for Nauvoo, where they arrived on the evening of August 6. Thus, though they hurried as fast as they could, a journey that today would take a few hours in an airplane took them almost two weeks.

The enemies of the Mormons were happy over the assassinations of Joseph and Hyrum Smith. They thought that the whole idea of Mormonism centered around and depended upon these two men, and that now the Mormons would disband. Even the Mormons themselves, in mourning for their leaders, were confused.

John Taylor, a Mormon who might have taken command, had been wounded by the same volley that killed Joseph and Hyrum, and it was thought that he could not live. Willard Richards, an apostle, did not care to assume authority until the rest of the apostles arrived and they could form a course of action.

Various people, who saw in disaster an opportunity to better themselves, were trying to put themselves in charge of all public property. This was a great deal, since most Mormons gave one-tenth of what they earned to the Church.

There were other people, some of whom were sincere, who saw the need for a leader and were trying to fill that need. The main struggle for leadership was between the twelve apostles and Sidney Rigdon.

Rigdon, who had been one of Joseph Smith's two personal advisers, thought that the mantle of leadership would naturally fall on his shoulders and he said so. He had influential Mormons to back his claims.

Parley Pratt, a staunch Mormon, kept leadership from being taken over in secret council. Largely owing to his efforts, it was decided that the people as a whole must vote on who should lead them. As a result, on August 8, a vast number of Mormons gathered around a temporary platform built for speakers.

For two hours and a half, standing on a wagon, Sidney Rigdon addressed the gathering.

He spoke with force of the Mount of Olives, battles, and almost everything else except the Mormons and their problems. Rigdon sought to accomplish by oratory what he could not do any other way. He had no real touch with the people; he was an actor on a stage and had very little to do with the people who stood before him or the many problems they faced.

When Sidney Rigdon was finished, Brigham Young arose.

Until now, Brigham Young had always been content to serve Joseph Smith, and to do as Joseph bade him. Only in this time of trouble did he emerge as the man he was.

For twelve years he had served the Mormons, always gladly. Often, as he himself expressed it, he had walked with "blood in my shoes" that he might serve more fully. But during those twelve years he had taught himself as much as he could about Mormons and Mormonism.

On this fateful day, the forty-three-year-old Brigham Young spoke to the people in language they could understand. With his calm, sure words and his forceful personality he literally held the vast gathering in the palm of his hand.

He cared not, he said, who led the Mormons. But were all their sacrifices, and all their hardships, in vain? Joseph and Hyrum Smith were dead, but the course they had laid out for their people would never die. Only their bodies were gone. The Mormons could elect anyone they wished to lead them, and they would still triumph as long as they held firm to the principles which they had followed so far.

When Brigham Young finished speaking, a vote was taken. Ten hands were raised in favor of Sidney Rigdon. All the rest voted to let the twelve apostles take over in Joseph Smith's place. Brigham Young was senior member of the twelve; for all practical purposes he had inherited the presidency of the Mormons.

He had, and knew that he had, succeeded to little except a crown of thorns. The enemies of the Mormons, enraged because the Mormons did not fall apart, would not stop their vicious attacks. But there were many things to be done. The terrible trip to the Rocky Mountains might be postponed until travel conditions were better. Joseph Smith had not indicated that his people must set out at once.

For the immediate present, there was a temple to be built and furnished. This was a place in which the Mormons might gather and worship. There were also numerous other undertakings. Though Nauvoo was already the finest city on the frontier, the Mormons wished to make it even finer. But the temple was the first consideration.

It was a magnificent structure that cost the Mormons more than a million dollars in money, but not all of this was given by the people in Nauvoo. By this time the Mormons had many converts throughout the Eastern states and in foreign countries. Some were wealthy and all gave what they could. The labor, of course, had to be done by those on the grounds.

While the temple was being built, again and

again Brigham Young proved himself a wise and just leader. Though he did not forget that his people must cling to things of the spirit, at the same time he knew that they must have things of the flesh too. It was right, he said, to sing and dance, for people could not give all their time to work. The ill, the old, and the weak could and did receive all they needed out of the "tithing," the one-tenth of everything which the Mormons gave to their church. But any men or women who were able to provide for themselves had to do so. If they asked for anything out of the tithing stores they were told to go to work, and there was plenty of work for all.

Meanwhile, the Mormons were still enduring persecution and the hatred of their neighbors. The authorities took a full part in this. Again and again warrants were issued for the arrest of Brigham Young and other Mormon leaders. However, no Mormon forgot what had happened to Joseph and Hyrum Smith, and few would submit to arrest. They knew that no Mormon would receive justice in the Illinois courts.

Such determination, backed by a willingness to act, proved to the border dwellers that the Mormons would not easily give up, and for a short period there was peace. During this time work on the temple and on various other buildings proceeded swiftly.

It was no use. More and more people came to Illinois and joined forces with those who hated the Mormons. Stronger and stronger their enemies became.

Finally all Mormons recognized the truth. They could not stay in Illinois but must, as Joseph Smith had said, plunge again into the wilderness and build new homes. The question was no longer should they go, but where should they go?

There were several places open to them: California, Oregon, Vancouver Island, the Salt Lake Valley. This last, about which he knew from reading General Fremont's account, probably held Brigham Young's interest more than any other place.

Again and again the Mormons had tried to

build homes for themselves. Again and again they had been driven from them. Suppose that, instead of traveling to some fertile country where there was sure to be trouble with settlers already there or those to come, the Mormons deliberately went to a desert which no one else wanted? Would they not have a better chance of living as they saw fit?

Meanwhile, the city of Nauvoo became one vast, bustling beehive of activity. Wagons by the score were built. Teamsters went in all directions to buy iron for tires and to strengthen other parts of the wagons. Seeds, fruits, and other provisions were gathered.

All through the fall and winter of 1845 the Mormons made ready for their mass migration. They were going into the West, an almost unknown country and certainly a savage one. All the luxuries of Nauvoo were to be left behind, and a good yoke of oxen would be worth its weight in gold.

In the bitter February days of 1846, the Mormons started.

3. The Start

IN ORDER TO HAVE A CLEARER UNDERSTAND-
ing of the mighty task facing the Mormons, it
is necessary to know something about their back-
grounds and the sort of people they were.

By 1846 Nauvoo was a good-sized city with
about twenty thousand inhabitants, most of

whom were Mormons. The population was further swollen by Mormons whose farm homes had been burned or who had been harassed by the mob. They had come into Nauvoo because they would be safer there. But, contrary to popular opinion, few of the Mormons were what we like to think of as the rough and ready frontier type, people who were accustomed to taking a rifle and a handful of salt and making a living in the wilderness.

They had gathered from every state in the Union and from many foreign countries. The greater number were gently reared, gentle-thinking people. All their lives many had been accustomed to the finest luxuries of the day. There were mechanics, artists, farmers, poets, teachers, editors, blacksmiths, and many other trades and professions represented among them. A number were college graduates, or had won honors at universities. Many had never shot a rifle, driven a team of horses or a yoke of oxen, and before coming to Nauvoo many had never seen anything that even looked like a frontier.

It was these people, and not a crowd of hardened pioneers, whom Brigham Young proposed to lead across two thousand miles of almost uninhabited wilderness to homes that would have to be built of materials at hand after they arrived. In addition, there were thousands of Mormons in the East and in Europe who wanted only an opportunity to join those already under Brigham Young. They did not care how far they had to travel or where they had to go in order to do so.

Brigham Young and the other apostles were trained and experienced in the ways of the frontier. They showed the more than two thousand families who were ready to move how to go about it.

Each family of five people was to have a strong wagon, six oxen to pull it, two cows, three sheep, one thousand pounds of flour, twenty pounds of sugar, a rifle with ammunition, a tent, seeds, farming and other tools, and

the innumerable personal articles such as needles, clothing, and soap, which any family needs
no matter where it is.

Brigham Young was also looking to the
future. The Mormons were going to live in a
wilderness, but it would be a wilderness only
until they had time to tame and civilize it. The
Mormon leaders knew perfectly well that, at
first, the people would have to live roughly and
would not have everything they needed. Nevertheless, the leaders had in mind something besides settlers' cabins. They determined from the
first that the Mormons were going west not only
to live, but to live well. They would build great
and wonderful cities, and everything necessary
they themselves must provide.

Therefore, the wagons also held flower seeds,
slips from fruit and other trees, grape vines, seed
potatoes, butter churns, saws, hammers and nails,
window glass, stone-working tools, lace for cur-
tains, and iron-working machinery.

Brigham Young further proved his intelligence and his great ability to look forward by asking every family that had a library to take at least one book which might later prove of worth to the entire community. A complete printing press, and everything necessary to operate it, must go along.

Brigham Young wanted much more. Sacred furnishings and the silver-toned bell from the temple, which even today may be seen in Salt Lake City, were to go with the Mormons. Two pianos and organs were in the wagons. Pitt's Brass Band and Duzett's band traveled with the emigrants. Brigham Young asked Mormons in England to send him surveyor's instruments and all the latest scientific instruments of the day in order that the Mormons might always be sure of their exact latitude and longitude.

Most Western travelers of the day—scouts, soldiers, trappers—would have laughed had they looked at the Mormon stores. But the usual Western travelers were not on the same mission as the Mormons. With few exceptions they went into the West to find profit for themselves; the Mormons were going to build homes.

There were many who thought, and doubtless hoped, that the Mormons would die on the trail. But Brigham Young, Heber Kimball, Parley Pratt, and other leading Mormons were determined to make the journey a success. There were two reasons why they were sure they would be successful.

First of all, they had complete faith in a God who would not desert them. Secondly, they had complete faith in themselves and their people. As little as possible was left to chance. They had the best wagons, the best gear, the best horses and oxen, the best maps, and the best plans that they could get. Probably, all things considered, they had the best people too. By far the greater number of the Mormons were not experienced frontiersmen, but they were intelligent and resourceful. They did not fear work, and hardship they could endure.

The first Mormons to leave Nauvoo, early in

February, were taken across the Mississippi on barges and flatboats manned by the Nauvoo Police Force. The immense wagons were driven onto the barges and lashed down so they could not move. Livestock were tethered so there was no escape. Crates of poultry were tied to the rear of the wagons.

For the first ones who left, this beginning step in their long journey was, perhaps, as dangerous and as breath-taking as any that was to come later. The weather, while not cold enough to freeze the Mississippi, was cold enough to form some ice. In addition, ice cakes that had frozen farther north were hurtling down the flooded river.

Ice smashed against the boats and barges carrying the people of Nauvoo. Mothers gasped as they gathered young children about them, while fathers and older boys helped with the oars. Horses and oxen lunged at their tethers. Chickens set up a wild cackling. Ducks fluttered in their cages and the honking of alarmed geese added to the general disorder.

So skillful were the river men, and so well had they planned, that the first companies of Mormons were taken across the wild river with the loss of only one span of oxen. Breaking their tethers, the fear-crazed beasts plunged across a flatboat and jumped into the river. Both were drowned.

That night's camp was probably as dreary and desolate a one as human beings have ever erected. Reaching the Iowa shore, the teamsters drove their wagons nine miles to a wooded area along Sugar Creek. Had there been any faint-hearted among them, they would have turned back the next day.

The temperature hovered near zero. There was snow on the ground and a freezing sleet falling. Of course nothing was prepared for the travelers and there could be little thought of comfort. The people who first crossed the river had to use all the skill and resourcefulness at their command just to stay alive through that terrible night.

There on the banks of Sugar Creek, that first night out of Nauvoo, the Mormons proved their mettle.

Some of the men busied themselves shoveling snow so that, though the best shelter they had was either a wagon or a tent, they would not have to sleep in the snow. Other men cut down trees and built great log fires to ward off the bitter cold. In addition to these, there were cooking fires that had to be built. Women who had never before cooked over such a fire, now took pots and skillets out of their wagons and proceeded to get a hot meal for their families. Those who did not know how to do it were taught by those who did. Only the very sick, the very young, or the crippled could rest.

Brigham Young and other Mormon elders moved quietly through the camp. These high officials put their shoulders to the wheels of

Many a woman had to learn the art of camp cookery.

mired wagons, paying no attention whatever to the mud, ice, and snow that spattered their clothing. They showed a man who had made a poor camp how to make a better one. More than once that night they knelt beside a cooking fire, took a skillet or a pot from the hands of a woman who had never before tried to cook anywhere but in a fine home, and taught her the knack of camp cookery. They comforted children and, when the camp was finally partly settled, Brigham Young and the other apostles appointed themselves as guards. That was too responsible a duty to delegate to anyone else.

That night, in what at the best was a primitive camp, nine babies were born. One mother lay on a rude bed in a sort of tent made with canvas walls that were thatched with bark. Freezing sleet was falling into the tent but other women stood about with pots, skillets, pails, and caught the sleet as it fell so that it could not touch mother or child.

The next day the camp on Sugar Creek was

organized. More and more families were coming in, and places must be made for them. What is more, they must be good places. The Mormons were going west, but they weren't going there in a slipshod, disorderly fashion.

Brigham Young was a sympathetic and understanding leader of his people, but he was no easy taskmaster. Strict sanitation and cleanliness must at all times be observed. The assembling Mormons were divided into companies, with leaders and sub-leaders for each, and every able-bodied person had appointed tasks which must be done.

By no means was it all work and no play. Brigham Young forbade drinking, gambling, and swearing. But in the evening, when the work of the day was finished, Pitt's Band could play for a camp dance. The camp had its quota of talented people—singers, jugglers, magicians—who helped entertain the rest. Books were so much in demand that often, passed from hand to hand, they were read by moonlight.

About the middle of February the Mississippi froze hard enough so that the ice would support a loaded wagon and the beasts that pulled it. The boats were no longer needed.

By the first of March, there was a whole city of tents on the banks of Sugar Creek.

4. Across Iowa

EVERYBODY AT SUGAR CREEK WANTED TO GO west, and reach the promised Zion, as soon as possible. Given their way, many of them would have started out cheerfully enough and at once. But most of these, if they did not die on the trail, would have had to turn back.

39

The Mormon leaders had understood clearly, and from the first, that this was to be no ordinary journey. Not just a few trappers' or traders' supplies, but a whole civilization, was to be torn down and loaded in wagons. Oxen and horses would pull it, at from five to fifteen miles a day, across a wilderness. Then the people would unpack and set up their civilization again.

Even today, with every modern means of transportation, moving a whole people and their belongings across known country would be no easy task. Then it was a hundred times more difficult and there were numberless problems which, today, would not exist at all. Brigham Young knew that the Mormons could do it only if all of them worked together, and there was much more than just the Sugar Creek camp which he had to consider.

There were about three thousand people in the camp. This left about seventeen thousand still in Nauvoo, and all of them had to be out by late spring. The Illinois authorities had said so. Aside from this, there were countless thousands in the East and in Europe who wanted to join the Mormons wherever they went. They must be received.

Only leaders of very great faith, courage, and intelligence would have dared even to plan such a thing. Now it was up to them to see that their plans did not go amiss, and Brigham Young was responsible for everything. Not only did he refuse to shirk the burdens laid upon him, but he planned with wisdom.

First of all, a message was sent to the Governor of Iowa. The Mormons were crossing the territory, the message said, and they wanted to cross peacefully. They asked no charity or help; they were well able to look out for themselves. However—at the time Iowa was also a sparsely settled frontier—it would be a very great advantage if the Mormons were permitted to plant crops on the public lands.

Brigham Young was thinking of the thousands still to come. Even a frontier did not have enough fish and game to support twenty thousand people, all of whom would follow the same route. Crops, food, must be there for those who had not yet started.

When he got permission to plant crops, Brigham Young placed Parley Pratt in charge of a small party and sent him on ahead. Pratt's mission was not only to locate good camp sites, but to find places suitable for growing crops. The Mormons planned to erect temporary villages at such places, with cabins and everything necessary for the use of those still to come.

The Mormons were reorganized into twelve divisions, with an apostle in charge of each. The divisions were further divided into hundreds, fifties, and tens, each with its own captain who was completely responsible for his group. Every man had an assigned task such as driving a wagon, building roads, cutting wood, hunting, or herding loose stock.

There were also men in charge of bridge-building, well-digging, road-making, house-building, and all the other jobs which such a large company might need.

The time came to leave Sugar Creek camp and make room for those still in Nauvoo. The great Western trek really began with a few wagons that struck across Iowa the last day of February. The following day almost five hundred wagons followed them.

It was at the same time a peaceful and a wild scene. At five o'clock the bugler roused the camp and, first of all, the people attended prayers. Then, while the women prepared the morning meal, lumbering oxen and frisky horses were brought in from wherever they had spent the night.

Often, just hitching the teams was a full-scale rodeo within itself. Horses that have run free are apt to be spirited, and many a bucking, plunging horse had to be dragged to its place in the team and held there by force, while the teamster who hitched him must be agile enough to dodge flying hoofs. Oxen, though good beasts of burden, can resent their masters. Many an ox-driver yoked his team with a wary eye on nervous hoofs or raking horns. The loose oxen, cattle, sheep, and horses had to be herded along.

At seven o'clock the bugle blew again and the company was under way, but not upon any hard-surfaced road.

The temperature was nineteen degrees above zero, just warm enough to soften the snow and let the heavy wagons plunge into the mud beneath it. The unfortunate beasts pulling the wagons sank in mud at every step, frequently so deeply that they could not even move, to say nothing of pulling the wagon. When that happened, and it happened often, the whole train was stopped while two or three extra teams were hitched to the mired wagon and it was hauled from its muddy bed.

Often a whole company could go no more than two miles in a day. At night they made camp, usually a wet one, and their only possible prospect for the next day was another struggle through mud and melting snow. If they traveled six miles, it was thought a wonderful journey.

Streams had to be bridged and roads built over otherwise impassable swamps. This was done by cutting a number of trees and laying them side by side to form "corduroy" road over which the heavy wagons rattled and bounced.

None of it was pleasant labor and all of it was hard. However, when there was such a job to be done, no hands were busier than those of Brigham Young himself. He might have commanded others to do it because, before leaving Sugar Creek, he had been sustained as "President over all the camps of Israel." This name the Mormons sometimes applied to themselves because they thought, correctly, that their migration compared to the flight of Moses and the Israelites when they fled from Egypt to their Promised Land.

Food was always a problem. The beasts of

burden alone required several hundred bushels of corn a day. While the Mormons were near the camp on Sugar Creek, they could get much of what they needed by trading at the frontier settlements or working for the settlers. The Mormons did anything they could honorably do.

In one day the members of Pitt's Brass Band split almost a hundred and fifty rails and took their pay in corn. That night the same band gave a concert in a frontier village and received, besides twenty-five dollars in cash, ten bushels of corn, a large amount of wild honey, and a free dinner.

The Mormons, like other people, had some personal possessions which they treasured greatly. Whenever possible they had taken these with them. Because so many of the Mormons were educated people, with a true appreciation of things artistic, many of these private treasures were genuine works of art.

The Mormons found it necessary to trade them for the necessities they needed. Many a tapestry, portrait, set of hand-painted china, or bit of jewelry, which today would excite the interest of any art collector, was left behind in a rude frontier village of the territory of Iowa. For them the Mormons got a few bushels of corn, a cow, an ox, a horse to replace one that had died on the trail, a new canvas cover for their wagons, or some of the numberless other things they needed.

As the travelers left settlements behind and reached Indian territory, getting just the necessities of life became more difficult. One night Pitt's Band, all the members of which had worked all day, played for an Indian chief and his dusky tribesmen. For this they received as much money as each member of the audience cared to give.

This money was added to as much more as the migrating Mormons could scrape up. Then it was given to a group who were going into Missouri, twenty miles away, to buy supplies. In addition to money, the foraging detachment took tables, dressers, furniture, and whatever else the Mormons could spare. They hoped to trade such things for all-important corn and bacon, of which Missouri had a bountiful supply.

Meanwhile, though the weary emigrants were delayed by mud, snow, flooded rivers and streams, and spring storms, they kept on. Sometimes a whole company needed most of their traveling day to cross a single swamp which might be a quarter of a mile wide. Sometimes they worked hard to travel one mile in a whole day. Rarely was nature on their side.

About the middle of April, the first of the wagons rolled into a place on the east fork of the Grand River, one hundred and forty-five miles from Nauvoo. They had buried many of their dead along the way, but there was no loss of heart among those who lived. They all set to work with a will to make this stop, Garden Grove, a village and farm land wherein oncoming Mormons might rest and renew their stores.

A hundred and ten men started making rail fences to enclose fields so that crops would be protected from wandering livestock. Forty-eight men built houses, ten dug wells, and ten devoted their time to building bridges. All the rest set to work plowing and cultivating.

Each family was to have started from Nauvoo with a year's supplies. However, many left Nauvoo with scarcely enough to see them through to Sugar Creek. This was because fields were destroyed, stock was shot, and other damage was done by vandals who wanted to take over what the Mormons left behind. More foraging parties were sent into Missouri, but it became increasingly evident that the migrating Mormons would have to provide for themselves as well as for those who were coming along.

At Garden Grove many hundreds of acres were planted to grain, many cabins were built, wells were dug. A small company was left to watch over everything while the main body pushed on. Twenty-seven miles west of Garden Grove, at Mount Pisgah, another such village was built.

Meanwhile, though warm weather brought hordes of hungry mosquitoes, the endless rains and snows ceased. The ground hardened. Instead of two or three, the Mormons were able to travel twenty miles a day.

This inspired such a spirit of confidence that many thought they might get to their Zion, their Promised Land—and nobody knew exactly where that was to be—before winter. Wilford Woodruff even recruited sixty men without families, who asserted that they were perfectly willing to go through to the Rockies that season and make things ready for all who followed. The Mormons were happy.

But again they were doomed to terrible disappointment.

5. Winter Quarters

IT WAS A TIME OF EXPANDING EMPIRES AND OF great unrest. Three nations—the United States, Mexico, and England—laid claim to land in North America, but boundaries were definitely settled only as far as the Mississippi River.

The United States, with a well-defined Canadian border as far as the Mississippi, had everything east of the Mississippi and a shaky claim to much of the territory west of it. England wanted what are now the states of Washington, Oregon, and parts of Montana and Idaho. Mexico laid claim to California and vast portions of what is now our own Southwest.

Texas, declaring its independence from Mexico, had been a nation in its own right. In 1845 Texas had ratified a treaty making her part of the United States, but her southern boundary was very much in dispute.

The Texans, now backed by the United States, insisted that their territory extended as far as the Rio Grande, or the same boundary that we have today. Mexico, equally firm, asserted that her territory reached north to the Nueces River.

In 1846, while the Mormons were on the trail, President Polk ordered the army to occupy the country south of the Nueces. Mexicans fired upon them, killing American soldiers, and the Mexican War was on.

Of this the Mormons, devoting all their energies and all their resources to their own westward trek, had heard only rumors. They had neither the time nor the inclination to pay attention to rumors; their own personal struggle could mean life or death to them and nobody knew it better than they did.

On June 14, almost exactly four months after they had left Nauvoo, Brigham Young and the advance companies of the Mormons arrived at the Missouri River, near the present city of Council Bluffs. All were in high spirits and very cheerful. Though they had been struggling through mud and swamps for almost four months, they were finally across Iowa.

They had learned much while crossing. Teamsters who had never done much except plow a field now knew how to take their teams almost anywhere. They knew what to do should an animal, or a team, become bogged down. Herdsmen had discovered how to keep a herd together in storms and gales, and how to urge them down a scarcely broken path. Mormon women were not only expert outdoor cooks, but had made improvements of their own in this art. A pail of cream, for instance, if tied on the back of a rumbling wagon all day long, would be churned into butter by the time the night's camp was reached.

Reaching the Missouri, the advance units stopped for a while. Ferries were built and used

to transport the Mormons across the river. Wagons were mended, rifles repaired, broken pots and kettles were patched. Weary horses and oxen renewed their strength in fresh, green pastures.

There was plenty of work to be done, but here at the Missouri camp the Mormons probably worked no more than about nine or ten hours a day. This must have seemed like a vacation after the sixteen or eighteen hours they had put in on the trail.

Every day more wagons gathered on the Missouri, and the camp was on both sides. Everybody knew, of course, that not all the wagons would get through to the West that year but all thought that some of them could.

Then the bombshell exploded.

Captain James Allen, of the United States Army, rode into camp and asked Brigham Young to raise a Mormon company of five hundred men to go fight in the Mexican War. Captain Allen said that he was acting under orders from General Kearney, and he produced credentials to prove it.

A greater disaster would be hard to imagine. At a time when the Mormons had many sick in their camps, and when they had desperate need of everyone who could do anything at all, certainly they could not spare five hundred able-bodied men. There were, however, certain favorable aspects.

The men were to receive arms, rations, and a small amount of money, which would be very useful to the Mormons. Brigham Young extracted from Captain Allen a promise that, if the Mormons raised the men, the army would molest none of the Mormon camps. In addition, the raising of such a force, to fight in California, would be clear evidence of the Mormons' loyalty.

Above and beyond all this, there was the matter of patriotism. Of the thirteen Mormon Articles of Faith, as written by Joseph Smith, the twelfth is this: "We believe in being subject to kings, presidents, rulers, and magistrates, in obeying, honoring, and sustaining the law."

Though few officials of the United States had ever done anything for them, the Mormons still believed firmly in their country and in the Constitution. Now their country was in danger and it had asked them for support. There could be only one answer.

Brigham Young himself took the lead in recruiting five hundred able-bodied men. Word was sent to the camps at Garden Grove and Mount Pisgah. The country needed men; the Mormons would furnish them. Brigham Young gave his personal promise to the men who enlisted that he himself would do everything in his power to see that their families did not suffer.

Accompanied by twenty wives of the enlisted men, the Mormon Battalion marched away on what was to be one of the longest foot marches in military history. Since then Mormons have fought, and died, in every war the United States has waged.

Losing five hundred of their best and finest men, the Mormons could have no thought of sending even an advance guard to the West in this summer of 1846. They could go no farther than the Missouri, and Brigham Young realized the great necessity of spending the winter right where they were.

There were about three thousand people already there. Before the summer ended there would be twelve thousand. Many, many more would be at Garden Grove, Mount Pisgah, and smaller villages which the Mormons had established along the way.

With characteristic energy, Brigham Young set to work. He went to Big Elk, Chief of the Omaha Indians. The Mormons, he said, must camp on the Missouri in the territory of the Omahas. They needed permission to cut trees, plant corn and wheat, and build houses. But, as usual, they asked no charity.

The Mormons had with them doctors, gunsmiths, blacksmiths. They had supplies which the

Omaha Indians could share, for were not all men brothers? In some places negroes were held as slaves, but the Mormons had negroes traveling with them and, far from being slaves, they had equal rights with the rest. If the Indians helped them, they would help the Indians. Both would profit, and Big Elk was quick to see that. He gave the Mormons permission to do as they wished and to stay on the Indian lands "two years or more."

This done, Brigham Young moved among his followers. Some, but not a great many, were crushed by this unexpected turn of events and the fact that they had lost five hundred of their best men.

Brigham Young told them not to worry. They were here, he said, and they could survive here. However, rather than weep in their wagons because they were afflicted, they must get out and work.

The dauntless spirit of one man overcame a multitude, and the Mormons responded whole-heartedly. Women whose men had gone off to war drove ox teams that skidded cottonwood logs to where houses were being built. Women helped build cabins, wielded axes, and did other men's jobs. Fields were plowed and planted. Before long the Mormons were referring to this place as "Winter Quarters."

Meanwhile, though most of the Mormons had abandoned Nauvoo, there were about a thousand of them left there. These were partly the sick and aged who could not go, partly people who had no way to travel, and partly those who hoped against hope that Nauvoo would be spared and that they would not have to move.

May 1, 1846, the final date set by the mob for complete evacuation of the city, came and went. The mob, intent upon pillaging the city, made their intentions known, and the Mormons remaining in Nauvoo appealed to the Governor of Illinois for protection. He responded by sending just ten soldiers under a Major Parker, who was later replaced by Major Clifford.

The mob became bolder. In September, led by a man named Brockmann, it stormed the city. Some of those who were able to flee did so. The remainder, under the command of a lion-hearted man named Daniel Wells, who was not then a Mormon but who later became one, prepared to defend themselves.

Four times the mob stormed the city. Four times they were driven back. Finally a truce was arranged. The Mormons remaining in Nauvoo were to be given an opportunity to leave. They did so, but not without further fighting and pillaging. Finally all the survivors reached the west bank of the Mississippi.

They were without goods and had almost no food. Many would have starved had not a near-miracle occurred. Thousands of quail were driven into the pitiful camp by a windstorm, and the hungry Mormons were able to catch them with their bare hands.

Hearing of the plight of these unfortunates, Mormons farther along the trail rushed relief trains back. Gladly they shared their own scanty stores with the survivors of the Battle of Nauvoo.

The last view these people had of Nauvoo, as they hit the trail west, was their sacred temple on the hill. The mobsters who had driven them out were looting it. Women and strong men alike wept unashamedly, and the train of wagons taking them west was a train of broken hearts. Then the Mormons lifted proud heads and not again did they look back.

Had the mobsters only realized it, theirs was a hollow victory and they had really destroyed very little. The real strength of the Mormons lay in the hearts, minds, and courage of the people themselves.

6. Into The West

THE WINTER OF 1846-47 PASSED PLEAS-
antly enough, with everybody busy. Part of this
was due to Brigham Young's insistence that busy
people are happy people, but there was plenty
to keep the winter-bound Mormons occupied.

Men repaired wagons, fixed old tools, and

made new ones. They looked for work, trapped furs, or hunted for wild meat, which was always a welcome addition to the Mormons' menu. Women, besides having a full-time job taking care of their families, were busy at their spinning wheels or with their knitting needles. Many women whose men had gone away to fight in the Mexican War had to take over all the jobs which, ordinarily, their men would have done.

It had been decided that Winter Quarters, as the community came to be known, would be a permanent stopping and resting place for all Mormons who were westward bound. Thus, it must be prepared for them.

That first season the Mormons built almost seven hundred houses, some few of sod but most of logs and all of them substantial. Schoolhouses were constructed. Blacksmith shops, a mill for grinding corn and wheat, and a sawmill were set up. The Mormons built a council house and a large public hall which served as a meeting place and as a place of worship.

Now that they were no longer on the trail, more and more men could go to frontier settlements and sell their labor, which was about all they had left that they dared sell. If they could not be paid in money for working they took corn, wheat, honey, bacon, and other foodstuffs. On the whole, food was more valuable. There was no place at Winter Quarters where money could be spent.

There was little real hardship or hunger that winter. Though the houses were not nearly so good as those left behind in Nauvoo, they were warm and weatherproof. Few of the meals were elaborate, and a dinner might be a bowl of cornmeal and a bowl of milk, but there was enough. The meals were pieced out with buffalo, venison, prairie chickens, and other wild meat that the hunters brought in. Cattle, sheep, and pigs could be slaughtered for eating only if they broke their legs, or were otherwise unfit for the trail. The Mormons realized the great importance of taking as much livestock as possible with them. When they reached their Promised Land, wherever that was to be, they wanted to rebuild their farms.

Not by any means was it all work and no play. When evening brought a lull in the labor, Pitt's Brass Band could play for another camp dance. Learned people among the Mormons lectured to others about various subjects. The younger people had a wonderful time riding horses, engaging in snowball fights, talking with or watching their Indian neighbors, having sleigh rides, and doing all the other things which youngsters will find.

Nevertheless, everybody from the oldest to the youngest knew that Winter Quarters was only a temporary camp, a mere stopping-place for the winter. On everybody's mind was the thought of the very long trail still to come.

All the Mormons who had come this far had some right to call themselves pioneers, but some took more naturally to life on the trail than others and among these were the ones who would have to go ahead. There were other reasons why certain men should be chosen as members of the Pioneer Company. Clearly, any man with five or six children to care for was better left behind. So was any man with an inferior team of horses, mules, or oxen. A man who cared to idle his time away could not go.

Brigham Young dared take nobody who would think of very much except getting through. The success of the whole venture, the future of twenty thousand Mormons already on the trail, depended on whether or not this group could succeed. They had to get through and, what is more, they had to get through in time to build houses, plant crops, and in other ways prepare for those still to come. A slip now could mean complete failure. Therefore, the first company had to be a picked one.

They were selected with great care. Besides having complete ability to take care of themselves in the wilderness, every man in this advance company had to have some skill which would be useful to the Mormons as a whole. Two blacksmiths with complete equipment were included. There were carpenters, farmers, mechanics.

Their equipment was chosen just as carefully. Aside from provisions for themselves and their beasts, they had twenty plows, ten drags for working the land after it was plowed, hoes, rakes, and other farming tools. They carried nails, hammers, saws, axes, and other tools. Every ox, horse, and mule had to be in the best of condition, and the pioneers did not forget to include an extra set of shoes, with nails, for each animal. They also had a cannon with which they hoped to frighten attacking Indians should that be necessary, and all the seeds they could fit into their wagons.

Finally chosen, the first company consisted of 143 men with Brigham Young himself at their head. Two of the men, incidentally, were Negroes. There were three women in the party: the wives of Brigham Young, his brother Lorenzo

Young, and Heber Kimball. The addition of two children brought the first party to 148 people. They had seventy-two wagons, loaded with everything they could take along, ninety-three horses, fifty-two mules, sixty-six oxen, nineteen cows, seventeen dogs, and some chickens.

The first party also carried the bell from the temple in Nauvoo. This had been cast in England by some of the finest artisans of the day.

Thomas Bullock was selected as clerk of the expedition, while Willard Richards and William Clayton would be historians. Brigham Young appointed Orson Pratt, who was later to become known the world over as a scientist and mathematician, to take charge of the scientific instruments which John Taylor had brought from England. Parley Pratt and John Taylor were left in charge at Winter Quarters, and later in the same year they were to follow the Pioneer Company with other Mormons.

On April 5, 1847, Heber Kimball took six wagons out of Winter Quarters. Two days later

Brigham Young and the rest of the Pioneer Company joined him, and again the march was on.

Some of the people in that first company had ability which came close to genius. It was very difficult at first to determine just how far they traveled in a day. William Clayton solved this problem by measuring the exact circumference of a wheel on one of Heber Kimball's wagons, calculating the number of revolutions that wheel would turn in a mile, and then counting all the revolutions in a day's travel.

Such a method proved too tedious. So William Clayton invented a set of wooden gears which, when fastened to a wagon wheel, would measure the revolutions for him. Thus, with surprising accuracy, the Mormons knew just how far they had traveled each day.

At the end of a day's camp, a wooden stake with the number of miles covered inscribed upon it was driven into the ground. When the Mormons could find no wood for such a purpose

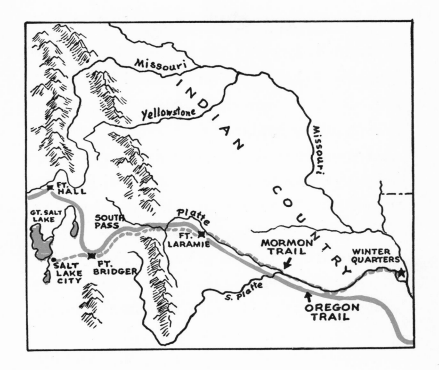

they used a buffalo skull. Like the trappers and travelers before them, they used these skulls in still another way. Aside from assuring those behind the Pioneer Company that "all is well," and recording the number of miles traveled, the skulls became convenient places in which to leave letters. Thus, a buffalo skull was one of the first prairie post offices.

Brigham Young had been advised to follow the old Oregon Trail, south of the Platte River. The Indians to the north, scouts had told him, were very warlike and would almost surely attack the Mormons. However, Mormon experience had proven to them that they got along better with Indians than they did with white men; few Indians were ever more savage than the mob that drove the sick and old out of Nauvoo. Reaching the Platte, the Mormons were undecided as to whether they should swing north of the river or stay south of it.

On May 3 the whole camp was called into conference. Though the Indians north of the Platte were burning the prairies, the immigrants decided to swing north and lay out their own trail. It became the "Mormon Trail," and so well did the advance party plan it that later, when the Union Pacific Railroad laid its cross-country line, the Mormon Trail was used as a roadbed.

While on the march, the Mormons had some

trouble with Indians who stole horses, tried to steal other things, and made various attempts to frighten them. However, the Mormons did not agree with some Western travelers who said that "the only good Indian is a dead one." Brigham Young himself said, "Feed the Indians. Don't fight them." Under the directions of their leader, the Mormons made every effort to be friendly with the red men. As a result, while on the march, the Mormons had little serious Indian trouble.

7. "Thousand Dollar Corn"

O N JUNE 1, BRIGHAM YOUNG'S FORTY-SIXTH birthday, the Pioneer Company came in sight of Fort Laramie. This was a rough fort which traders and trappers had erected on the Platte River, and it was hundreds of miles from any civilization. But there was no time for a birthday cele-

74

bration, and probably Brigham Young himself was the last to think of or wish for such a thing anyhow. There were other more important things to be done.

William Clayton calculated that they were about five hundred and fifty miles from Winter Quarters, and that the Pioneer Company had been on the trail almost exactly seven weeks. However, even though they had come this far without losing a single person, it had been anything but an easy journey.

They had been harassed by Indians to some extent. They had weathered buffalo stampedes and they had seen a vast number of bears which frightened their horses, oxen, and mules. Wagons had broken down; beasts of burden had become sick or injured. Nevertheless, there was no thought of anything save going on.

The country to the north of Laramie was impassable by wagon. So the company had to cross the Platte and travel on the Oregon Trail for a while. The man in charge of Fort Laramie,

James Bordeaux, rented them a flatboat for fifteen dollars, and with this the Mormons took their wagons and goods across the Platte.

Bordeaux treated the wayfarers very kindly, letting them camp wherever they would in or near the fort and making the full accommodations of this frontier outpost available to them. He also warned them that two companies of Missourians, under command of their old enemy L. W. Boggs, had recently passed over the trail and were bound for Oregon.

It must be supposed that these meetings with trappers and traders who knew the country were very important to the Mormons. Though they had supplied themselves with the best maps available, these maps were not so accurate as the ones we have today. A river, an important landmark, or even a mountain range, might be out of place. By talking with people who had been there, Brigham Young was able to correct errors in the maps he had been able to get.

It must also be supposed that, possibly even before they left Nauvoo, Brigham Young had decided to seek a permanent home for his people somewhere in the Salt Lake Valley.

The Oregon Trail was so crowded with Western home-seekers that, often, a hundred wagons a week went through. All of these people wanted to go to Oregon or California. To say nothing of settling in or near the Salt Lake Valley, many of them feared even to cross it. According to some reports it was unfit for any humans except a rather retarded tribe of Indians who were already living there. Anybody else who tried to make a home in the Salt Lake Valley would certainly have a struggle.

If this were true, and according to the best information of the day it was, why would Brigham Young even think of settling in such a place?

Aside from what he had read in the few accounts that were available, or learned by talking with trappers and traders, he knew nothing whatever about the Great Salt Lake or the country around it. Certainly he had never been there. But there must have remained within him bitter memories of the constant strife which had been the Mormons' lot so far. Like Joseph Smith, he wanted peace for his people, and peace he would not find if he took them near anyone else.

The Mormons believe that Brigham Young had a divine revelation which told him to take his people into the Salt Lake Valley. However, he also understood the people he led.

The Mormons had been told that it was impossible to live at Nauvoo; then they had taken the swamp that was Nauvoo and made it into a beautiful garden spot. They had already performed what others thought was impossible. They were very hard workers, and Brigham Young must have felt that if any Indians at all could make a living in the Salt Lake Valley the Mormons could do it too. Beyond any doubt there were places where an easier living could be had, but the Mormons were not looking for a life of ease. It was much more important to them to have peace so that they might think and worship as they chose.

At Fort Laramie there were a few Mormons awaiting the Pioneer Company. They were members of the Mormon Battalion who, for various reasons, had been detached from the Battalion and sent to Pueblo, Colorado, to spend the winter. There were a company of Mormons from Mississippi and others from the Battalion still in Pueblo. Brigham Young sent four men to bring these people to Laramie and thereafter to follow the trail laid out by the Pioneer Company.

The Pioneer Company pushed on, and there must have been a grim sort of humor in the minds of many as they did so.

The Oregon-bound Missourians just ahead were the selfsame people who had mistreated the Mormons in Missouri. But at that time the Mormons had had women and children to care for. Now they were a company of strong, well-armed men. Would the Missourians, under Boggs, the former governor who had told the Mormons to get out of Missouri or die, feel like another fight? The Mormons would not have been completely human if at least a few among them did not hope to catch the Missourians in a fighting mood.

Fortunately there was no battle. Instead, about a hundred and forty miles out of Laramie, at the second crossing of the Platte, the Missourians hired the Mormons to ferry them over the river. A Mormon named Ira Eldredge had built a remarkable skiff—a boat capable of carrying almost two thousand pounds—out of sole leather. Cleverly constructed, until it was needed the boat had served as a wagon box.

Now it was put to the use for which it had been intended. The Missourians were ferried across the Platte, paying for their ride with flour, grain, and meal. Thus, and in spite of the fact that there must have been a few men with itchy trigger fingers watching the operation, in the middle of the wilderness the Mormons had their supplies renewed.

Nine men were left at this ferry. Their principal purpose was to carry oncoming companies of Mormons across. But Brigham Young also hoped that, by ferrying Oregon-bound pioneers, they would earn supplies to help the Mormons through the approaching winter.

The main body of the Mormons went on. On June 28, near the headwaters of the Sweetwater River, there occurred a meeting which, had there been any cameras to record it, would forever be a classic of historical photography. Jim Bridger rode into the Mormon camp.

Bridger, one of the most colorful characters in frontier history, and perhaps the greatest Western scout of all time, had spent almost his entire life in the wilderness. One of the original Mountain Men, he knew Indian camps, warfare, horses, snow-capped peaks, buffalo trails, beaver pelts, and rifles much better than some city dwellers know their own cities. Bridger had forgotten more about pioneering in the West than some so-called scouts and pioneers ever knew.

It is not known what he thought as he swung from his horse and strode forward to meet Brigham Young. Perhaps he was contemptuous of this soft-spoken, God-fearing man who thought he could lead a company into the Salt Lake Valley and settle there. During his twenty-five years in the West Jim Bridger had seen many wagon trains come through. Later he had seen, hanging in some Blackfoot or Pawnee lodge, many scalps of those who made up the trains.

Perhaps, as many had been, Jim Bridger was overcome by the strength and forcefulness of Brigham Young.

Certainly he gave the Mormon leader priceless information about the Great Salt Lake, or "Utah Lake," which Jim Bridger himself had discovered. Floating down the Bear River into Great Salt Lake, Bridger had tasted the brackish water and thought himself in an arm of the Pacific Ocean. Later he had corrected this impression. Fifty or more times, said this man of the West, he had visited Great Salt Lake.

Of one thing Jim Bridger was positive: No crops would ever grow in the Salt Lake Valley. So certain was he of this that he himself would give a thousand dollars for the first bushel of corn anyone could produce in such a country.

8. "This Is The Place"

ON THE SAME DAY THAT THE FIRST COMPA-
nies left Nauvoo, a party of 235 Mormons led
by Samuel Brannan sailed from New York on
the ship *Brooklyn*. They reached San Francisco,
then called Yerba Buena, on July 29, 1846.

Almost a year after arriving there, Samuel

Brannan crossed the snow-locked Sierra Nevadas to meet the west-bound Mormons. He met them at Green River, Wyoming, on June 30, 1847, and he was taken at once to Brigham Young.

It was another very dramatic meeting. Brigham Young had been on a rough trail for almost a year and a half. Brannan, accompanied by two companions, had dared high mountains, deep snows, Indian-infested wilderness, and wild animals, to come to this meeting with the leader of all the Mormons.

That night, in Brigham Young's personal camp, the fire burned until the light of a new day dulled its glow. Samuel Brannan and Heber Kimball must have been present. So were William Clayton, Willard Richards, Orson Pratt, and others high in Mormon councils. Beyond them crowded as many Mormons as could find room.

None of them was, in any sense of the word, a servant to Brigham Young. All of them were strong, forceful people who, under any and all circumstances, would speak their minds and advance their own ideas. It made no difference whether they disagreed with their leader. No matter who led them, men like that would not be silent if they thought they should speak and had something to say. All listened intently to Samuel Brannan.

Come to California, he urged. It was truly the Golden Land. There was no persecution there; Californians did not care how a man worshiped, or if he worshiped, provided he was a man. Not only were all of the 235 who had sailed on the *Brooklyn* prosperous, but all were prospering beyond their wildest hopes. There was room in California for all Mormons and anyone else who cared to enter. The soil was matchless, the climate superb. Opportunities were boundless. Why even think of settling in the Salt Desert when California beckoned?

To the trail-weary Mormons, the picture Samuel Brannan painted must have been entrancing. But all of those listening had been first-hand

witnesses of the intolerance of Palmyra and Kirtland, the fighting at Independence and Nauvoo.
They had had rich lands there too, until someone else wanted them. Brigham Young's reply
to Samuel Brannan summed up the feelings of
the whole company:

"Let us go to California, and we cannot stay
there over five years. But let us stay in the
mountains, and we can raise our own potatoes
and eat them; and I calculate to stay here!"

These were not a braggart's empty words.
Brigham Young had weighed in full measure
the problems facing the Mormons; not again did
he intend to have an Independence or a Nauvoo. The reference to raising and eating their
own potatoes was symbolic; Brigham Young
meant that the Mormons would get along very
well as long as they were left alone, and it was
better to be left alone on a desert than to accept someone else's orders in a paradise.

The answer was final and the Pioneer Company pushed on toward the Great Salt Lake.

Jim Bridger was perhaps the greatest of Western scouts.

When thirteen more men from the Mormon Battalion joined them, and also joined Samuel Brannan in his glowing picture of California, the Mormons were not swayed from their purpose. Brigham Young even turned a deaf ear to his brother, who pleaded with him to go to California and not to think of settling in "such a barren, God-forsaken country as would be found in the Rocky Mountains."

The trail they were on had been traveled, but largely by scouts and trappers who had had only horses and mules with them. Horses and mules could go where wagons could not, and the Mormons had to devote much of their time to building a road.

It was not a road as we think of it. The Mormons might be following a stream bed, and several drivers with ox or mule teams would be sent ahead to pull the biggest boulders out of the way. Men with axes might follow to cut trees, or to fill deep holes with stones. The Mormons did not ask or expect an easy ride, they wanted only to get their wagons through. Just the same, road-building alone was a vast enterprise.

They stopped at Fort Bridger, which they reached July 7, to repair wagons, shoe draft animals, and let weary beasts and men rest. Two days later they were rolling again, on into the eastern slopes of the Rocky Mountains. Near the head of a place called Echo Canyon—a canyon in the Western mountains is similar to a valley in the Eastern—Brigham Young came down with mountain fever. This is a serious disease caused by the bite of a small insect that lives in the mountains.

Those with him were greatly concerned. Mountain fever was a terrible illness that had brought death to many; only in comparatively recent years has a serum been discovered that will prevent it. However, Brigham Young was less concerned about himself than he was about the success of the Mormons as a whole.

He could not move, but there were those who

could. Summoning Orson Pratt to his sickbed, Brigham Young asked him to take forty-two men and twenty-three wagons and, at all costs, to get through to the Great Salt Lake Valley. Winter was coming and, should there be no more men than those already in the Pioneer Company, the approaching winter was sure to be a desperate one. Crops must be planted, houses built, and everything possible done to meet nature on her own terms.

Orson Pratt was a young man. He was resourceful, completely devoted to the Mormon cause, and he had an inexhaustible energy. The previous year the ill-fated Donner Party, who later had become marooned in the High Sierras and had had to resort to cannibalism just to stay alive, had come this way. Orson Pratt wanted, if possible, to find and follow the Donner Party's trail.

Pratt's task was not an easy one and he knew it. The group had already climbed part of the way into the Rockies, and no Mormon had ever encountered travel like this before. It was far different from the prairies or the gently rolling Eastern mountains. Nothing in the travelers' past experience would help solve the problems that now faced them.

Nevertheless, where old ways failed they invented new ones. If they brought their wagons to a place where the trail dropped so sharply

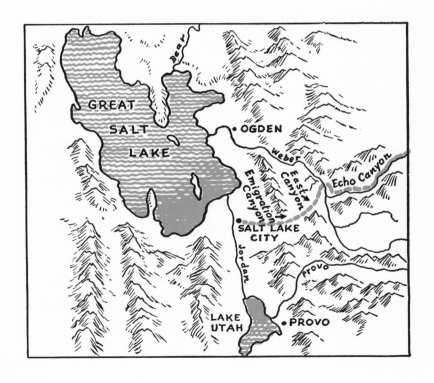

that any wagon trying to go down it would surely be wrecked, they built the trail up with whatever materials were at hand. By this time they had moved so many stones, boulders, stumps, and fallen trees that they were past masters at such labor. They were not the inexperienced people who had left Nauvoo; any teamster could look at any place and decide in a split second whether or not he could take his wagon up or down it.

Descending steep slopes, they chained the wheels so that they could not turn and thus transformed their heavy wagons into sleighs. Even with chained wheels the draft animals had little to do; the sliding wagons were on their heels all the time.

On the Donner Party's trail, they went down Echo Canyon and up East Canyon. Often, with the instruments he carried, Orson Pratt took their elevation. Frequently they were almost a mile above sea level, and still the rocky peaks towered above them.

The trail swerved to Big Mountain. The travelers climbed. From the summit of Big Mountain, on Monday, July 19, 1847, they saw in the distance the Western mountains. Between them and that far-off, entrancing horizon lay the valley of the Great Salt Lake, but they were still a long, hard way from it.

They descended Big Mountain and hit the trail to what was later called Emigration Canyon. It was there, on July 21, that they were overtaken by Erastus Snow.

Erastus Snow, Brigham Young's trusted adviser, brought messages to Orson Pratt. The advance party was to bear north as soon as they were in the valley. There they would find a cool stream, and they were to camp near it. Erastus Snow could not explain how Brigham Young knew of the existence of this stream, but he did not question its presence.

Perhaps a scout had ridden into camp and told Brigham Young about the stream. But it is certain that, in just getting an advance party into the valley of the Great Salt Lake, the Mormons had already performed a miracle. Even though the Mormons themselves were courageous, efficient, strong, and resourceful, only the very cynical can doubt that they were helped by more than human wisdom.

Orson Pratt and Erastus Snow decided to go ahead of the rest and scout the country. They climbed a butte, or small, flat-topped hill, and were overcome by what they saw.

The valley stretching before them was desolate and overgrown with sage. But the Great Salt Lake stretched in the distance. They saw willow-fringed streams sparkling out of the mountains. Fed by melting snow, the streams flowed constantly.

In the whole valley there was just one lone, sad tree. The withered remnants of this are preserved today at Salt Lake City.

Erastus Snow and Orson Pratt rode back to the wagon train with joyful news of their discovery. They guided the wagons down, and took them to the creek that flowed from the north. On July 23 they camped on the ground now occupied by the Salt Lake City and County Building.

There was, first of all, a camp to set up. Two hours after their arrival, the advance party had their teams hitched and were trying to break the hard ground with their plows. They succeeded only in breaking their plow points. Then they remembered more of Brigham Young's advice.

"Throw a dam across the creek," he had told Erastus Snow, "and let the water soak the earth. It will then be soft enough to plow."

Irrigation of land was not new; its basic principles were known to people who lived long before Christ. But this dam across City Creek was one of the first links in the irrigation systems which have reclaimed so much waste land in the United States. Two out of five of our agricultural acres would still be useless were it not for life-giving water brought by irrigation; and the Mormons began irrigating the day they arrived in the Salt Lake Valley.

Meanwhile, though he was still very sick, Brigham Young insisted upon going on as soon as he was able to move. Riding in a light wagon driven by Wilford Woodruff, he bounced and jolted over the hard trail laid out by the advance party. The rough road made the illness that had gripped him more serious, but he was the leader of the Mormons and he could not rest.

When Woodruff's wagon climbed a low ridge, Brigham Young asked that it be stopped while he looked over the Salt Lake Valley. Then he pronounced the words which will forever live in American history:

"This is the place. Drive on."

Again the Pioneer Company was together. Wilford Woodruff, carrying a bushel of seed potatoes in his wagon, vowed that he would not rest, eat, or drink, until he had plowed a field and planted them. By one o'clock that July 24 afternoon he had fulfilled his promise.

This was the first humble trickle of a mighty flood of good things which were to flow from the state of Utah.

9. The Beginning

THE AVERAGE PERSON TODAY, UNLESS HE IS
a farmer or is in some way connected with farming, not only has nothing to do with the produc-
tion of his own food but gives little thought to
where it comes from.

The Mormons, however, knew very well that they would have to feed themselves or starve. Therefore, on the very afternoon that the Pioneer Company again assembled, every plow was busy. The two blacksmiths with the Company set up their forges and anvils right in the open and repaired the plows that had broken. Before night, wheat, corn, buckwheat, and other seeds were planted, as well as potatoes.

The Pioneer Company had been supplied with some of the choicest seeds the Mormons had, and it was most important to get some into the ground. So, the plowmen were busy from the first light of morning until darkness made further labor impossible. Other Mormons were on the way, and they would have to eat.

At the same time, the Mormons were practical farmers and the season was very late. Their crops should have been planted two months before, and there was some doubt as to whether those they were planting now would yield any harvest at all. Therefore, they did not plant all their seed but only as much as they thought they could spare.

The best was saved for the next year's planting. It was very valuable. Seed could be replaced only after a long, dangerous journey that, under the best of conditions, would take months. Therefore, a bushel of seed corn or wheat was far more precious to the Mormons than a bushel of the purest gold. One of the first things those who were not plowing did was construct a safe place for their seed. It had to be a dry place, for wet seed spoils; and it had to be a place where rats, mice, squirrels, and other vermin could not enter.

All through the 23rd and 24th of July the plowing and planting went on. On the 25th, Sunday, the Mormons rested. No Mormon objected to working the clock around, if necessary, on any other day. But there was to be no work on Sunday.

Instead, they gathered in their camp to worship. After the services, Brigham Young offered some fundamental rules to guide the colony.

Any person, he said, might come here to live and he need not be a Mormon; even though few people had ever been tolerant of the Mormons, the Mormons must have tolerance for others. So Jews, Gentiles, Mohammedans, heathens, and anyone else who sought a home might find it here. However, anyone who came must have respect for the Mormons and their beliefs. There was to be no private ownership of water rights, but they were to belong to all. No man who came here to live would be asked to pay for farm land; if he wanted a farm it would be given to him and he might till it as he saw fit. But he must not let it lie fallow or fail to till it. Nor should any man be asked to pay for a city lot.

This reference to city lots might have sounded silly to one who did not know the Mormons. They were in a desolate valley, far from any civilization, and as yet they had only the rude wagons in which they had arrived. Nobody had had time to build any kind of a house. But even before they left Nauvoo the Mormons had decided that, wherever their long trail ended, they would build a great and wonderful city.

Busy with plowing, planting, digging irrigation ditches, and getting their camp in order, the Mormons had also lacked time to find out very much about the valley into which they had come. It was very important that they do some exploring as soon as possible.

On Monday, July 26, several parties went out. Even though he had not yet recovered from mountain fever, Brigham Young himself went with one party. On July 27 they had a bath in Great Salt Lake and, to their astonishment, found that it was impossible to sink. The salt in that lake makes it much easier for a body to float there than in fresh water.

They also climbed the mountain that rises above the hot springs and named it Ensign Peak. It is known by that name to this day.

Gathering at the main camp, the exploring parties compared notes and thus gained some idea of the sort of country they had found. They knew where the land was good and where the best grazing was to be found. They had seen herds of antelope, mule deer, elk, and mountain sheep. Some of the explorers reported good stands of timber in various side canyons. They knew where the best water flowed. All this was very important because, unless they knew, they could not make sound plans.

Of all the places they had seen, the best possible site for a city seemed to be the one where their camp stood. Some of the members objected to making a hasty decision about anything so important and wanted to do more exploring. Brigham Young was anxious that all be satisfied, but he was sure that they would find no better place for a city. After a while the rest agreed.

It is quite important to understand that the Mormons took possession of all they had found not in the name of their church, but in the name of the United States of America. At the time, Utah was claimed by Mexico.

When all had agreed that the site of their rude camp was an ideal site for their city, they went about planning it.

Never far from their minds was the fact that they must build another temple. On July 28, Brigham Young, the eight apostles with the Pioneer Company, and the clerk Thomas Bullock walked northward to a place about half-way between the north and south forks of a stream which the Mormons called City Creek.

Brigham Young thrust his walking stick into the ground and declared that in this spot the temple would stand. Wilford Woodruff drove a stake to mark the place. Today the Mormon Temple, one of the most beautiful in the world and one which has attracted visitors from all over the world, stands on that very location.

The Mormons planned their capital with a vision and wisdom that has gone into the planning of very few American cities. The city was to be divided into blocks of ten acres each, with streets eight rods, or a hundred and thirty-two feet, wide, running at right angles. Brigham Young could have had no knowledge of the automobile traffic to come but, because he insisted on wide streets, Salt Lake City is one of the very few American cities that today can handle automobile traffic without the usual traffic snarls and jams.

As soon as the plans were laid, Orson Pratt started surveying. He also made other observations such as taking the latitude, longitude, and altitude. Though the instruments at his command were the finest to be had at the time, they were crude compared with what we have today. Nevertheless, later scientific checking on Orson Pratt's observations proved that he was amazingly accurate.

Though only three women had started from Winter Quarters, six more had been among the Mormons awaiting the Pioneer Company at Fort

Laramie. They, too, had made the long, difficult march from that point on. On July 29, the Mormons already in the valley were joined by those of the Mormon Battalion and Mississippi Mormons who had awaited at Pueblo. The newcomers brought with them sixty wagons, a hundred horses and mules, and three hundred cattle.

The arrival of this party brought the population of the Pioneer camp up to about four hundred people. The Battalion members immediately built a bowery, a building thatched and walled with willow and cottonwood to serve as a place of worship and for public meetings.

It became necessary to provide housing. Many of the men were plowing, planting, digging irrigation ditches, exploring, building roads into the canyons for lumber, or otherwise busy in some good cause. Brigham Young asked those who were not doing these things to help him make a fort. As usual, he himself led by setting a good example. An expert carpenter, he not only used all carpenter's tools but patiently taught those who did not know how to use them.

Brick-makers set to work making adobe, or clay, bricks. Teamsters hauled logs from the canyons. Men with picks and shovels leveled the earth. As usual, everybody except those who were too sick to work toiled from morning until night.

When completed, the fort was a rectangle of houses joined together. The walls were twenty-seven inches thick at the base and the outer wall was nine feet high. One wall was made of logs, the other three of adobe brick. Each house had a loophole facing the outside so that, if the fort were attacked, the defenders would have some place from which to shoot. Windows and doors faced the inside. There were heavy gates which were locked at night.

Shortly afterwards Samuel Brannan, disappointed because the Mormons insisted on staying here, left to return to California. Captain Brown, who commanded the portion of the Mormon Battalion that had been at Pueblo, went with him to collect the men's mustering-out pay, to carry messages to that portion of the Battalion still in California, and to bring back things which the colony would find useful.

Not in vain had Brigham Young been chosen leader of the Mormons, and certainly he was not a leader who led from an armchair. Under his guidance, and without the loss of a single person, the Pioneer Company had reached their Promised Land, their Zion. There were other companies on the way, following the plainly marked trail, but by far the greater number of Mormons awaited at Winter Quarters.

Brigham Young might have asked someone else to go get them. But he had given his solemn personal promise to bring the Mormons through; it was he upon whom everyone else depended.

On August 22, he left the colony in the

charge of John Smith, an uncle of Joseph Smith, and began the long journey back to Winter Quarters in order that he might fulfill his promise to his people.

10. The First Winter

OTHER WAGON TRAINS, ALREADY ON THE
way, were following the long, slow, hard trail
laid out between Winter Quarters and the tiny
fort which the Pioneer Company had built in
the wilderness. One by one they arrived. The
last train, carrying 150 people led by Jedediah
Grant, came in October. Then advancing winter

closed the trails to wagon travel, and the 2,095 people who had reached the site of what is now Salt Lake City dug in for the season.

Besides the fort, their wagons, their tents, and a few personal possessions, the settlers had their weapons and about five thousand horses, mules, cattle, sheep, pigs, and goats. They had brought with them a few hundred chickens, a few dozen pigeons, some hives of bees, and some dogs. There were many hundreds of bushels of corn, wheat, potatoes, buckwheat, and other food supplies stored in various places.

But by far the greatest and most valuable things owned by the Mormons in that forsaken valley were the courage in their hearts and the strength of their characters.

There were none weak or spiritless among them. Most people who hadn't the heart to face what the Mormons must face had turned back long before they reached Mount Pisgah. The rest had turned back from Winter Quarters. Those remaining—and there were many women and children among them—were just the people to face a difficult situation and to solve knotty problems.

Planted too late, the crops over which the Pioneer Company had labored so hard were almost a complete failure. Few vegetables ripened. Potatoes were so small that it would have taken three dozen just to satisfy the hunger of one healthy man or woman. It was better to save them for future seed than to eat them.

Almost all the grain they had must be saved for seed. Brigham Young had gone back to Winter Quarters, and before leaving he had promised that next year he would guide thousands more to the Promised Land. He would depend upon those already there to have a harvest in order that those to come might eat. Plainly they could not plant their grain and eat it too.

They did have some wheat that they dared grind into flour and some corn for corn meal. John Neff ground this in a mill which he had built on Mill Creek. It was at the best a rough mill, and not yet properly set up. But John Neff had transported the machinery for it all the way from Nauvoo, and when the next summer arrived he hoped to have a proper grist mill.

The Mormons in Salt Lake Valley were not entirely cut off from the rest of the world. The trail back to Winter Quarters was well marked, and every ten to fifteen miles there was a box or a buffalo skull. A Mormon who might be looking for stray horses would go back on the trail. Always he carried a sheaf of letters which he would leave in a box, or inside a buffalo skull, along the trail. Perhaps the next day, perhaps not until a week later, a wandering trapper would ride the trail, pick up the letters, and leave them in the last box or buffalo skull he reached. Then someone else would pick them up and take them farther. In this way, there was some correspondence between the camp in the Valley and Winter Quarters.

The Mormons in the Valley devoted themselves whole-heartedly to advancing the plans for their colony. With only horse, mule, and ox power, and hand plows, they had cleared and plowed almost five thousand acres of land before the ground froze. This would be a big undertaking with power tools; with the tools available to the Mormons it was an enormous task.

Hundreds of acres were sown to wheat and rye, as both are crops that can be planted in the autumn and harvested early the following summer. The Mormons continued to dig irrigation ditches so that water might flow into their thirsty land. Two wings were added to the fort, and more houses were built. Some few hardy souls, confident that they could take care of themselves, built houses outside the fort.

Woodcutters were busy in the canyons, and men driving oxen and mules dragged the logs down to the colony. Fences were built so that, once the fields were growing, wandering livestock would be unable to destroy the crops. Hunters went out to get deer, elk, mountain sheep, and antelope.

Throughout the hard winter the Mormons never lost sight of their bright dream and their great plan; and an ambitious plan it was.

Mormonism, Brigham Young hoped, would attract hundreds of thousands of converts. Not all of them could live in the Salt Lake Valley, spacious though it was. Much more land was needed.

It is doubtful if, in that year of 1847, even Brigham Young knew how much territory the Mormons should claim. But two years later the boundaries of "the state of Deseret," which is

Boundaries of "the state of Deseret" are shown in color.

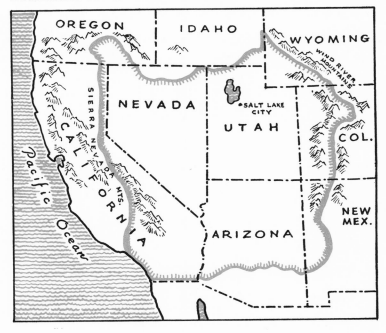

what the Mormons called their empire, were clearly set.

Besides all of Utah, Deseret included the southwestern part of Wyoming, parts of southern Idaho and Oregon, great chunks of Colorado and New Mexico, all of Nevada, almost all of Arizona, and about the southern third of California, including the seacoast up to where the city of Los Angeles now stands.

That first winter nobody knew too much about any part of Deseret, and it was very important that exploration continue. The biggest trip was made by a party of eighteen Mormons led by Jefferson Hunt.

They left Salt Lake City in November, only about four months after the Pioneer Company arrived. Their purpose was to explore the country and to visit one of the huge ranches in southern California. There they hoped to be able to buy additional livestock as well as seeds, plants, and other things the Mormons needed.

Because they knew that it was impossible to cross the High Sierras in winter, they took the southern route. However, they took provisions for only thirty days and the trip required forty. Hunt's party survived by killing and eating three of their saddle horses. Eventually they arrived at a ranch some thirty miles south of the present city of San Bernardino.

Here they bought forty bulls, about two hundred cows, some horses, some seeds, and then started back. All the bulls and more than half the cows died before they returned to Salt Lake City, but Hunt's men had had an opportunity to see southern California and to open the way for later Mormon colonization in that area.

Meanwhile, the hard-pressed colony at Salt Lake City was almost without anything to eat, and getting clothing of any sort was almost as difficult as getting food.

With typical Mormon skill, the settlers solved these problems. There were no wild vegetables growing in the area, but there was an abundance of a plant called sego. The Mormons found that the root of this was both good to eat and nourishing, and they dug great quantities of it. Thistle tops, normally scorned as an article of food, were not only found to be good but actually became one of the staples used at every meal. They had milk from their cows, a few eggs from their chickens, and once in a while a beef animal was slaughtered.

There was almost no flour with which to make bread, and a grand dinner of that winter of 1847-48 is described by John Young, Brigham Young's nephew.

"I was a herd boy, and while out watching the stock, I used to eat thistle tops until my stomach was filled. At last the hunger was so sharp that thistle tops would serve no more. Father took an old bird-pecked ox-hide from the branch of a bush that stood on our lot, and made from it a delicious soup. This was enjoyed by the whole family as a rare treat."

At long last the end of what seemed an endless winter drew in sight. And the spring brought another great emergency.

11. The War Of The Crickets

THE FIRST YEAR—THE WINTER OF 1847-48—
the settlers in Salt Lake City lived the grimmest
sort of existence. Not only was there little en-
tertainment of any kind, but just getting what
they needed to keep themselves alive was a
struggle.

They kept their faith that a great city would rise here and a great empire would grow around it. Though they had to live one winter in houses with leaky roofs, though the snow and rain dropped upon their most treasured possessions, the future was bright with promise. They had spent one year in a mud-thatched shack. Very probably the next year would bring them a house not much better. But the future still held promise. Within five years most of them would be living in houses as fine as those they had left behind in Nauvoo.

Though there had been some deaths in the colony, the very fact that most of them survived the winter was proof that they were winning. They had done this much. They could do the rest.

No longer was there need to cringe from wintry blasts, or to shrink from rain, sleet, or snow. The sun shone every day, and new life was the order.

Soft buds appeared on the willows. The sego lilies, which had helped keep the colony from starving, wore green foliage. Long-legged, awkward colts ran beside their mothers in the horse herds. Cows thrust anxious muzzles at new calves, and frisky lambs played their own games in the sheep pastures. Chickens became very secretive about their nests and, on the brimming irrigation ditches, ducks and geese sported and courted.

It was a gay and happy time, as final freedom from winter always is. But to these self-exiled people, who had given up almost everything they owned in order to create new homes in the valley of the Great Salt Lake, it was especially gay and happy.

Best of all, their crops showed every sign of succeeding. The thousand acres they had planted to winter wheat showed fresh and green above the plowed land. This alone meant salvation. Even if the crop was not of the best quality, that much wheat was sure to yield a good harvest and much of it could be ground into flour. This, in turn, would mean life-giving bread. The next winter there would be no living on thistle tops and sego roots.

As soon as the ground could be worked, the Mormons started cultivating the rest of the five thousand acres which they had already cleared, plowed, and fenced.

Corn, potatoes, peas, lettuce, melons, every possible sort of grain and vegetable, was planted. The Mormons proved all over again that, if water can be brought to it, the harshest desert soil will often yield the finest and tenderest crops.

Every person who was not desperately needed for something else worked from morning until night planting and tilling the fields. And for the first time it seemed as though, at last, the pendulum had swung in their favor.

Last year the five thousand acres had grown

nothing but sage. This year, thanks to life-giving water, it was green with food crops. If they were even moderately successful, there would be enough to feed all the people in the valley and all those who could possibly get there this season. The time of desperate want was behind them.

Then the plague struck.

The year before, the Pioneer Company had discovered that, besides various wild animals and Indians, the valley was the home of numberless crickets. They were not the cheerful little insects that are famous for chirping on hearths, but big, fat creatures that weighed more than a quarter of an ounce.

To the Mormon Pioneers, who did not then suspect the damage they could do, the crickets were a nuisance. The women, tidy housekeepers, disliked them particularly because they got in their improvised cupboards, crawled over their clean clothes, and even got in the food.

The native Indians caught vast numbers of them and used them as food.

In the spring of 1848 a wave of crickets came down from the mountain sides to attack the Mormons' growing crops.

At first, though they seemed like a horde, their numbers were nothing compared to what came later. First of all they bit off and ate the leaves of the young fruit trees which had been set out.

Even this was a matter of grave concern. Those trees had arrived there the hard way. For a year and a half, and over two thousand miles, they had been tenderly cared for and nursed in order that they might grow when, finally, a place to plant them was found. Boys with sticks and brooms were set to guard the fruit trees, and to beat back the crickets as they came. But a dozen new ones appeared for every cricket that was destroyed.

Even so, until the growing rye and wheat

started to ripen, the crickets seemed to be at the very worst an especially loathesome pest. Then, with the forming of the grain on the stalks, the trickle of crickets became an overwhelming flood.

Like flowing lava they poured from the mountain sides into the grain fields. There were countless millions; it was impossible to step anywhere without crushing crickets. But, as though they were issuing from some place that had a never-ending store of them, more came on.

They would climb a stalk of grain, bite off the head, let it fall, and then descend to eat it. There could not have been a more grave situation. The Mormons had lived through one winter with almost nothing, but the coming season would bring thousands of additional settlers. They could not possibly survive another season without grain. Even in Independence or Nauvoo they had not had enemies more deadly than the crickets.

Everybody in the colony turned out to fight them. Fields in their path of advance were burned, and the ashes were scarcely cool before the field was hidden beneath a new wave of hungry crickets intent on the grain. Deep ditches were dug. The crickets filled them with their own bodies, and the living crossed on the dead.

The earth seemed alive with crickets. Millions were crushed with clubs, brooms, and sticks. Millions more took their places. The horde needed only a few minutes to go through and destroy a whole field of grain, and there was nothing the Mormons could do to stop them.

For the first time there was deep despair. John Smith, still in charge of the colony, was advised to send a messenger to Winter Quarters and tell Brigham Young to bring no more people to the valley. If more came they would certainly starve, for there would be no grain for them.

John Neff, who was building up his grist

mill, went to John Smith and told him bluntly that he would not go on. Already, he said, he had put a great deal of time and money into his grist mill. Now he might better take it apart and move elsewhere because certainly there would never be grain to grind here. For the first time Brigham Young's followers began to doubt his wisdom in bringing them to such a place.

Brigham Young, however, was a keen judge of men. He had placed John Smith in charge of the colony not because he was related to Joseph Smith, but because within himself he was a strong and capable man who would know how to handle emergencies. And now John Smith rose to this one.

Under no circumstances, he said, would he send a messenger to Brigham Young and advise him to bring no more colonists. The Mormons would not fail. He also pleaded with John Neff to continue with his grist mill. There would be grain and the Mormons were not going to starve. Then John Smith called upon the one Refuge that never failed the Mormons; he summoned all the people to three days of fasting and prayer.

Much of the fast-ripening grain remained on the stalks when the Mormons heard a sharp cry. It was about three o'clock in the afternoon, and as one person they raised their heads to determine the source of the cry. They saw what they thought was an unbelievable horde of pigeons.

But it was a vast flock of sea gulls that lived on Great Salt Lake. By the countless thousand they came, and dropped into the cricket-infested fields. At once they began to eat, not the grain, but the crickets. More gulls came to join those already in the fields.

Thereafter, with the first light of dawn, the gulls came back to the fields until all the crickets were destroyed, and the crops were saved.

Ever since then, the sea gull has been a revered bird to the residents of Utah. A monument to it stands in the temple block at Salt Lake City.

12. The Empire Grows

MEANWHILE, BACK AT WINTER QUARTERS,
Brigham Young had been very busy. On the
Iowa side of the Missouri River the Mormons
who had stayed behind had built a large log

building, called a tabernacle. This would seat about a thousand people, and all business meetings were conducted in it.

At one of these meetings, Brigham Young was promoted to President of the Church—he had been "President over all the camps of Israel"—and Heber Kimball and the gentle Willard Richards were chosen as his personal counselors, or advisers.

Advice was sent to every Mormon missionary —and they were scattered the world over—to gather all Mormons who had been driven from their homes and send them to Winter Quarters. Whatever they had they were to bring with them, and gold was very acceptable because that would buy things the Mormons needed.

However, though many of them proved themselves excellent businessmen and bankers, the possession of gold was never the Mormons' foremost aim. If they hadn't any gold they were to bring "anything that grows upon the earth that will please the eye, gladden the heart, or cheer the soul, of man. Bring the best stock of beasts, birds, and fowl, and tools of every kind."

If they hadn't this much, or anything at all, they were just to bring themselves. Brigham Young had always believed that the greatest wealth, and the only real wealth, was the people themselves. Nor did they have to be Mormons.

When the Catholic missionaries came to Salt Lake City, Brigham Young gave them a sum of money and a site upon which they might build their church. To the early Jewish Congregation he gave not only money and land, but the use of the Mormons' own meeting house in which they were free to hold services until their synagogue was built.

It is interesting to note that in 1870, almost eighty years before the present nation of Israel was established, Brigham Young sent a mission to Jerusalem to proclaim that land the true home of the Jews.

It is entirely possible that, after the assassination of Joseph and Hyrum Smith, the Mormons would have disbanded had they not had a man as strong as Brigham Young to hold them together. Much of his success was owing to the fact that he had a broad and sweeping mind which was not capable of petty thoughts. Always he advised his people not to waste their time trying to tear other peoples and their religions down, but to build themselves and their religion up.

Brigham Young also told those at Winter Quarters to move across to the Iowa side of the Missouri and establish a settlement there. All who were too sick or too old to travel, and all who did not want to travel, could make a handsome living there and provide a stopping place for Mormons still to come.

The settlement was named Kanesville in honor of Colonel Kane, an army officer who admired the Mormons greatly and who had done

much for them. They had also done much for
him. The first year at Winter Quarters Colonel
Kane had been brought in suffering from a
raging fever. He had been tenderly nursed by
the Mormons, who beyond any doubt saved his
life.

After the Mormons moved west the name of
Kanesville was changed to Council Bluffs, and
by that name it is still known.

There can be little doubt that Brigham
Young's heart lay largely with the settlement
he had started in the Salt Lake Valley. He was
eager to lead more colonists to it and, in May
1848, the main body of the Mormons still at
Winter Quarters started their trek.

They traveled in three companies, commanded by Brigham Young, Heber Kimball,
and Willard Richards. Almost 2,500 people,
with 750 wagons and an unbelievable number
of horses, mules, cattle, sheep, pigs, goats, and
other creatures, followed the trail laid out by

the Pioneer Company. Records reveal that there were even four turkeys, five ducks, one crow, and seven squirrels with them. Probably the crow and the squirrels were children's pets.

Their journey did not differ greatly from that of the Pioneer Company except that, being larger, the wagon trains traveled more slowly. They were further handicapped by having with them a great number of old and very young people who had no able-bodied person to see to their welfare. The men who ordinarily would have cared for them had died or been killed, or were serving with the Mormon Battalion, or had been sent to work elsewhere for the Mormons. However, true to his word, Brigham Young did not abandon these near-helpless beings. Rather, he insisted that they be considered before anyone else.

On September 20, 1848, the first of these new companies arrived at Salt Lake City. Before winter forbade travel, all came safely in. By

the autumn of 1848, there were about five thousand people in the valley of the Great Salt
Lake.

The arrival of so many new people made
many new problems. The Mormons never had
had enough able-bodied men to do all the work
that must be done, and many of the converts to
Mormonism were women. The country was a
rough frontier where raiding Indians, or even
Mexicans, might come at any time. Though the
women always contributed their full share to
the Mormons' progress, in such a country and
at such a time there were some tasks that they
simply couldn't do. They needed the protection
offered by a rifle in the hands of a straight-
shooting man, and they needed the food that a
man could grow or find better than they could.
It would have been very difficult for a woman
to live alone. Therefore, since there were more
women than men, the practice of plural marriage, or taking more than one wife, was firmly
established.

Plural marriage was not, as some think, to blame for the early persecution of the Mormons. Joseph Smith first spoke of it to his clerk, William Clayton, in 1843, long after the Mormons were driven out of New York, Ohio, and Missouri. It is also true that any Mormon who took more than one wife had first to prove his ability to provide for them. In spite of the fact that the idea had the full approval of the Church, fewer than five per cent of the Mormons took more than one wife.

Non-Mormons did not approve of the idea at all, and there can be no doubt that Utah would have been a state much earlier had the Mormons not practiced plural marriage. However, one of the articles of faith as established by Joseph Smith reads, in part, "I believe in honoring, obeying, and sustaining the law." Since having more than one wife was against the law, the Mormons themselves did away with it. Today no true Mormon believes in or practices plural marriage.

There had been a harvest, but due to late spring and early autumn frosts, and the cricket plague, it was not nearly so plentiful as the Mormons had hoped. It was evident from the first that, though nobody would starve during the winter to come, there would be nothing to waste. And there was much to be done.

There were about 450 buildings, most of which were houses. John Neff, heeding John Smith's words, had kept working on his grist mill and it was in very good order. For cutting trees into lumber, there were three sawmills already in operation. Fences were built around fields, and more sage had been plowed out to make new places for raising crops. A great deal had been done.

But still there was a great deal to do. Even 450 houses would not accommodate 5,000 people, so more had to be built. The Mormons all worked together to achieve a common end, and when there was not enough to go around, what there was had to be shared equally. By no means, however, did they intend to smother the will of the individual to work for himself.

Therefore, lines that marked clearly every man's property must be determined. One man who wanted to work hard might clear, plow, and irrigate fifteen acres. A second might cultivate only five acres of his allotted farm. In a time of emergency, which the winter of 1848 remained, a man with a plentiful harvest might be called upon to share with those who had less.

But clearly it was unfair to ask him to continue to do so. When the colony prospered—and nobody doubted that it would—those who were willing to work hard should not be asked to share the fruit of their labor with men less energetic. So every person had to be given due credit for the work he did.

There were schools to build and teachers to be selected for them, crops to harvest and thresh, wheat and corn to grind into flour and corn meal. Firewood had to be cut, lumber sawed, hay cut and stacked. There were also, in that autumn of 1848, other settlements with which contact must be maintained.

The year before, 1847, Perrigrine Sessions, Samuel Brown, and Hector Haight searched for better grazing lands for their large herds of cattle. They went north, into the present Davis County. The next year others moved to the north and became the first settlers of Bountiful, Farmington, and other towns in Davis County.

Early in 1848, Captain James Brown, who must have prospered in California, bought from a trapper named Miles Goodrich the land where the city of Ogden now stands. The price was three thousand dollars and, aside from the land, it included seventy-five head of cattle, various other things, and one cat.

Little by little some Mormons moved away from their original fort, this time not to explore the country around them but to settle it. Before the end of 1848 there were fifteen colonies instead of only one in the State of Deseret. None of them was very large, and none was very far from the original fort. But every house a Mormon built pushed the wilderness back that much farther.

13. The Mormons And The Indians

EVEN BEFORE THEY LEFT NAUVOO, THE MOR-
mons were perfectly aware of the fact that they
would have to travel through Indian country
and that many of the Indians were unfriendly.
Brigham Young took this into full account, and

he planned accordingly. As usual, he planned intelligently.

Many of the men on the westward trail in that day were violent men given to quick action rather than thought. They had been taught to hate all Indians, friendly or otherwise, and they did all they could to hurt the red men. They would kill men, women, and children, and often their only reason for such murders was that they were killing another Indian. This vicious policy, and the mistaken idea that "the only good Indian is a dead Indian," probably did as much as anything else to encourage the terrible Indian wars.

The Mormons never gave support to the notion that Indians must be kept peaceful by terror or force. It was, as Brigham Young said, cheaper to feed them than it was to fight them. In addition, the Mormons were very tolerant of all peoples. All had the God-given right to think and do as they saw fit as long as they hurt nobody else.

144 THE COMING OF THE MORMONS

But not even the Mormons could escape all Indian trouble.

The first fort was a safe place, and it could be defended against almost any Indian attack. But it little suited the Mormons' adventurous spirit to be confined in a fort or anywhere else. One of the first to move out was Lorenzo Young, a brother of Brigham Young.

He was advised not to go for, if he went, he put himself and his family in danger of being massacred by Indians. However, Lorenzo Young had brought his family west to farm, and not to huddle in a fort. He built and moved into a cabin on City Creek. Lorenzo Young and his older sons left the cabin to till their fields. Behind them they left Harriet Young, Lorenzo's wife, and a newborn child.

The men had barely departed when, without bothering to knock, an Indian pushed his way into the cabin and demanded food. The frightened young woman gave him all she had. The Indian ate and requested more, but she had

no more and she told her unwelcome guest so.
At once he fitted an arrow to his bow, bent the
bow, and pointed the arrow at her heart, all the
while speaking fiercely.

Harriet Young could not understand his language, but his actions were plain; she could find
more food or she and her baby would die. In
this great crisis her courage did not fail her,
and she thought as calmly as she could.

Lorenzo Young had not left his wife and baby
without protection. Before leaving the fort he
had bought a huge and savage dog, and the dog
was chained in the cabin's other room. Signal-
ing to the Indian that he must wait, Harriet
Young went into the room, untied the dog, and
urged him to attack.

The raging beast hurled himself through the
doorway straight at the man. Before the Indian
had time to shoot his arrow the dog had hurled
him to the floor and would have killed him had
not the young Mormon wife come to the rescue.
She dragged the dog away and chained him.

Then, instead of killing the helpless man on the floor, she dressed his wounds and let him go.

The Mormons' way of life could not help producing many hard-riding, hard-fighting, hard-living men who at the same time knew how to get their way without a fight. Some of the finest Indian scouts in the West were Mormons and, though it would be difficult to choose the best one, Jacob Hamblin might qualify for that honor.

Hamblin was directed by Brigham Young to take a party of Salt Lake City merchants through to California. As soon as he got the order, he hurried to overtake the wagon train, which had already started. He found a group of Indians who had captured a white man. It was their intention to torture him because, they said, they "wanted a little fun." Nobody except a scout who knew all about Indians and their ways could have talked them into freeing their captive, but Hamblin did.

The two caught up with the wagon train and

Quietly Hamblin gathered the hostile Indians around him.

found it surrounded by hostile Indians. Again Hamblin took charge. The Indians wanted the merchants' horses and oxen. But if the merchants lost their animals—their means of transportation—they were lost too. Hamblin solved this problem very wisely. He knew that the Indians were a people of great honor, who would not break their pledged word. Calling all the Indians around him, he said that the white men's beasts of burden were faint from lack of food, for the white men did not know where to find good grazing. Would the Indians take the animals out to graze, and give their word of honor to bring them back? The Indians agreed. In the morning, without one missing, every horse and every ox was returned.

Farther on, Hamblin got word of a war party that intended to attack the wagon train, kill the men, and take their goods. Again, with only his smooth tongue and a few presents, Hamblin persuaded them not to attack.

Thus, without firing one shot or endangering

one life, this Mormon scout prevented what might have been a massacre.

There would always be some red men, just as there would always be some white men, who were born troublemakers. So, although the Mormons wished to live at peace with the Indians, and though they tried to do so, they could not avoid all Indian wars. The most serious clashes resulted because of a long-practiced custom of the country.

For many years it had been the habit of Mexican traders to come into Utah with horses, guns, and cheap trinkets, and to trade them for Indian women and children. These were taken back to Mexico and sold into slavery.

It was a very profitable trade for the Mexicans; in Mexico one slave might buy them fifty horses or twenty-five guns. But from the very first most Mormons had hated slavery in all its forms. In 1852, after Brigham Young became the first Governor of Utah Territory, he had the Legislature enact a law providing that Mormon families could, by force if necessary, take into their own homes all Indian children who were to be sold into slavery in Mexico. The children were to be taught some useful trade, and after they had learned it, they were to be set free to practice it.

This enraged the Mexicans. They knew that the Mormons were hard and terrible fighters once they had decided to fight for what they thought was right. The Mexicans did not dare attack the Mormon colonies openly. Instead, they encouraged the Indians to attack.

There followed a period of great uncertainty. No Mormon, leaving his house to work in the fields, could be certain that he would not have to defend himself against raiding Indians. No house was ever left unguarded. The Indians stole horses and cattle. Mormons in lonely settlements had to leave their houses time after time and gather in a fort to beat off an Indian attack.

Mormon scouts like Jacob Hamblin, as hardy

and courageous a group as ever rode the West, prevented many massacres. Always they brought warning to some threatened settlement, and enabled the Mormons to prepare for their own defense.

Then one Pedro Leon, a Mexican trader, announced his intention of coming into Utah to trade as he saw fit. He had a trading license signed by the Governor of New Mexico, which was still Mexican territory, and he intended to trade in Indian women and children.

In terms that left no room for doubt, Brigham Young warned him. Anyone at all might come into Utah with trade goods, horses and mules, cattle, or anything at all that would be good for the public, and nobody would stop him as long as he acted with decency. Anyone who came into Utah with the intention of trading in human beings would be arrested, and the least he could expect was a jail sentence.

This aroused Walkara, Chief of the Ute Indians. He thought that the Indians had a right to sell their women and children if they wanted to, and he did not intend to let the Mormons interfere in what he considered Indian affairs. Walkara declared open war.

The Mormons did not want war, but they would not tolerate slavery and they were quite willing to defend themselves. Mormon scouts were always out. Men went into the forests with an ax in one hand and a rifle in the other, or they carried rifles while they guided their plows. There were various battles in which some Mormons were killed, but the Indians usually got the worst of it.

Finally, and as usual acting first and thinking afterwards, a party of California-bound emigrants, who might have passed peacefully through Utah, killed one and wounded two Indians in the Sevier Valley. Their anger at white heat, the tribesmen rode the warpaths with the idea of killing any white man they might find. Unfortunately, they found Lieutenant John Gunnison, an army engineer who had never hurt anyone at all, and his party of surveyors. At once the Indians attacked.

Pierced by more than a dozen arrows, Lieutenant Gunnison fell almost immediately. His eleven men put up a brave fight, but when another party of surveyors, under Captain R. M. Morris, reached the scene and beat off the attackers, only four of Gunnison's men were alive.

This tragedy saddened all of Utah. Lieutenant Gunnison was not a Mormon, but he was a quiet, well-behaved man who wished only to carry on his engineering work. He was liked by all the Mormons, and was welcome in their homes.

Brigham Young, Gunnison's friend, was heartbroken. But, as usual, he saw that it would do no good to sit idly by and weep. The Indian war must end. Brigham Young himself headed a wagon train that set out in search of Walkara

They found the Indian camp and rode into it. A man of great personal charm, Brigham Young talked to Walkara.

The proud chief, under the spell of Brigham Young and further lured by a promise of presents, was willing to bury the hatchet. The fact that at least two Indians had fallen for every Mormon that had been killed might have helped him make up his mind.

Shortly afterwards Brigham Young was visiting the Mormon settlements with a group of his companions, when he received word that Walkara was again ready to go on the warpath. The Leader of the Mormons did not hesitate; if another Indian war was brewing, the time to stop it was now.

Again, and fearlessly, he rode into Walkara's camp. He found the Indians very hostile. A favorite child was dying, and Walkara demanded that Brigham Young give one of his party over, so that a white man might be killed and accompany the dying child to the Spirit Land. Nothing else would do. Outnumbered, in the midst of enemies, the white men were in a very dangerous position.

Then Brigham Young asked to see the child. There is no written record that he gave it any medicine, but Brigham Young was a practical man who would not have hesitated to use anything which he thought might help the child. He also called upon Divine help, and the child recovered.

From that time on, Brigham Young and Walkara were fast friends.

The Mormons had other Indian troubles, but not nearly so much as did settlers in other sections. Their policy was one of tolerance and understanding. They truly believed that the Indians were their brothers and they acted accordingly. Because they did, they got along very well.

It is a remarkable record.

14. The Echo Canyon War

THE FIRST GENUINE PROSPERITY, OR GOOD times, that came to the Mormon colony resulted from the great California gold rush of 1849. Gold had been discovered at Sutter's Fort, and the news went around the world as swiftly as wind-driven fire travels through dry grass.

As usual, rumor outsped the truth. All anyone had to do in California, or so some reports went, was to provide himself with a shovel and enough boxes to contain the gold that he could dig out of the creeks. Everybody would be a millionaire in very short order. People really believed such things and acted accordingly.

Sober New England storekeepers, who had been able to make a comfortable living, invested their savings in horses, oxen, or mules, and started for California. So did doctors, lawyers, soldiers, mechanics, farmers, teachers, and people from every walk of life. There was little sense in working for a living when, in California, one might become rich overnight.

The Western trails were crowded with wagons, people riding every sort of beast that was able to carry them, and people on foot. Prices rose to unheard-of heights. In Salt Lake City, still a long way from the gold fields, a single bushel of potatoes might bring as much as twenty dollars. Anyone able to get the potatoes over the mountains might sell them in the gold fields for a dollar apiece.

The one thought was to get to California and the gold, and the Mormon settlements in Utah now offered the best route. As far as the Missouri, everything east of Utah was wilderness. So was almost everything west of it. Only in the Mormon settlements was there a chance of buying fresh supplies, or of trading weary, worn-out animals for fresh ones. People came by the thousands.

There is, perhaps, a moral in this that may be very well applied to the problems of our day. Though they certainly tried hard, the Mormons discovered in 1849 that they could not be isolationists, or live in a world all their own, either!

Many California-bound gold-seekers, finally reaching Salt Lake City, threw both caution and sense to the winds. They might have driven

The California Gold Rush brought visitors galore.

loaded wagons this far, but now that they were so close to gold the important thing was to get over the mountains and start digging. So they traded everything they had for fresh, strong horses and enough supplies to get them over the mountains.

Thus, more than a thousand miles from the nearest settlement, the Mormons fell heir to a vast amount of goods which the gold-seekers sold cheaply. Many articles of clothing, furniture, and food were cheaper in Salt Lake than they were in New York City.

Though they were closer to the gold than anyone else, and might have reached it before anyone else, few of the Mormons took part in the gold rush. They were home-builders, not adventurers, and Brigham Young expressed the wish that, if there was gold in Utah, it would not be found. If it were, it would bring an even greater horde sweeping in and, though crops were more plentiful, there was still not enough to feed a vast number of people. He did encourage the Mormons to look for iron, coal, and other things they could use.

While the Forty-Niners went on over the mountains, the Mormons stayed at home and planted their crops.

By 1850, only three years after the Pioneer Company had reached the site, Salt Lake City had a population of about 6,000. There were as many more people in various other settlements. The Mormons had almost 17,000 acres planted to grain, and that year they harvested about 130,000 bushels of wheat, corn, and rye. Their livestock was valued at more than a half-million dollars, which is a substantial sum even now and was a huge fortune then.

Salt Lake City had sidewalks, and trees of various kinds were growing along its wide streets. There were many shops and stores, and several hotels. The *Deseret News,* today one of the most influential papers in the United States, was established with Willard Richards as editor. A small but beautiful tabernacle and a Council

House had been built. A good government had been set up, and all this had been done at the expense of the Mormons themselves.

Long ago the Mormons had petitioned the Government at Washington to admit their state of Deseret, which means honey bee, to the Union. In 1850 their request was partially heeded. They were admitted as a territory under the name of Utah, after the Ute Indians, instead of Deseret.

Brigham Young was appointed the first Governor. However, now that Utah was officially a territory of the United States, United States officials must help govern it. Several were sent to Utah.

In 1850, as at all other times, most of the people serving the Government were fine and honorable, with a strong sense of duty. Unfortunately, there were a few who had no sense of duty and not much of any other kind, and they were among those sent. The conscientious officials, or those who wished only to perform the duties of their office, got along very well.

The others, those who took it upon themselves to force the Mormons to change their religion and those who saw in their offices an opportunity to enrich themselves, fared differently.

They found Salt Lake City far different from Nauvoo. In Nauvoo the militia, or soldiers and police, had helped persecute the Mormons. Here the only militia were Mormons themselves. Given an order which was contrary to the well-being of the Mormons, they would not obey it.

These officials took the only revenge they could. Finding that the Mormons refused to be plundered, or to change their ways, they sent to Washington reports that were little better than deliberate lies. The Mormons, they said, were conspiring against the United States. Anyone who challenged a Mormon would be killed. The Mormons burned official books and documents and had no respect for the officials sent to govern them. These and similar reports continued to come to Washington, and they were believed there.

Meanwhile the Mormons were going about their business, which was building up the land they had settled. They brought in great numbers of new settlers, including many companies who pushed hand carts all the way from Winter Quarters. They continued to establish new towns, and worked their farms.

In the year 1857, nobody was more surprised than the Mormons themselves to discover that a force of 2,500 soldiers was coming to put down a rebellion against the United States. They had a right to be surprised, for the rebellion existed only in false reports submitted by evil officials.

Three scouts, who rode five hundred miles in a little over five days, brought the news. Its effect was to set all of Utah ablaze.

Brigham Young, as Governor, issued an order that under no circumstances were any army troops to be permitted to enter the territory. He sent a protest to Washington.

Four times the Mormons had been forced to abandon their homes and move. This time they also intended to fight. They did not want a war, but they would accept one before they would again accept what they had been through at Independence and Nauvoo.

A party of Mormons under the same Daniel Wells who had set up a defense of Nauvoo met the army at Fort Laramie. As they passed it they burned Fort Bridger, which the Mormons had bought from Jim Bridger and put in use as a supply depot.

Reaching Laramie, the Mormons burned some army wagon trains, set fire to the grass and, in surprise night attacks, kept the soldiers constantly on the alert. They were under strict orders from Brigham Young not to kill anyone and not to shoot at any soldiers. They did not have to.

As the army advanced, the Mormons re-treated. But, instead of green pastures and the stores at Fort Bridger, the army found only burned prairie and the fort in ashes. Their animals could not graze and they had only scanty reserves of food. Furthermore, they realized that they could not fight their way through the rugged mountain passes under such conditions. The army was forced to make a winter camp.

In September, Captain Van Vliet made his way alone to Salt Lake City. It was a courageous thing to do for, according to the reports he had, the Mormons were cutthroats and robbers.

Nevertheless, Captain Van Vliet was cordially received. An intelligent man, he had only to look about him and to talk with men like Brigham Young, Willard Richards, and John Taylor, to know that the reports circulated about the Mormons were untrue. He still warned the Mormons that, though they had stopped the army for this year, next year enough reinforcements

would be sent to overwhelm the Mormon defenders.

That might be true, the Mormons replied, but
when the army came let it bring plenty of supplies, for none would be found here. Every
house would be burned, every field destroyed,
and every tree cut. Joseph and Hyrum Smith
had yielded themselves to the army. Not again
would a Mormon do it.

Meanwhile, Colonel Thomas L. Kane, whom
the Mormons had befriended at Winter Quarters, received the protest Brigham Young had
sent to Washington. At once he left the city,
sailed down the Atlantic coast, crossed the Isth-
mus of Panama, and went up the Pacific Coast.

He made his way overland to Salt Lake City
where, because he wanted to see for himself if
the Mormons were really rebellious, he introduced himself as "Doctor Osborne." Without
question he was taken into the house of Mormon Elder William Staines, who did not know

that he was really Colonel Kane. There he was given the most generous hospitality. Colonel Kane knew then that the Mormons were neither rebels nor villains, but his old friends of Winter Quarters.

It was a very harsh winter, with much cold weather, and there was such small possibility of an army crossing the snow-locked passes that the Mormons did not even bother to post a guard. However, small parties could get through.

Colonel Kane volunteered to travel to the army camp and get in touch with Governor Cumming, who had been sent under protection of the army as Utah's new governor. He persuaded Governor Cumming to travel with him, and without military escort, back to Salt Lake City.

Governor Cumming was received as courteously as Colonel Kane had been, and Brigham Young himself introduced the newcomer as Governor of Utah. But Brigham Young still remained as President of the Mormon Church and his order remained unchanged; no troops were to come.

However, President Buchanan had signed an order that troops were to enter the territory. General Johnston, in command, intended to enforce that order. At length, with Brigham Young's agreement, an arrangement was made.

The troops were to enter the territory, but were not to stay in Salt Lake City or near any of the settlements.

Just to be sure that the army kept its word, once again the Mormons fled. Ten years of the hardest kind of work had gone into building their fine capital city and the farms around it. But, driving their livestock ahead of them, southward they went. Many of them found a temporary refuge with Mormons at Provo and other southern settlements. Brigham Young himself, moving out of his mansion, camped in a hut which had served as a house for a tame bear.

June 26, 1858, the army marched out of Emigration Canyon into the city. But the only

Mormons now in Salt Lake City were grim-faced men who, with ready torches, crouched behind the shuttered windows of houses that were piled high with straw. Should the troops show the least sign of stopping, the torches would be applied to that straw. Other Mormons, men who wanted peace but who had more than once proven their ability to fight, were prepared to set fire to growing crops, to chop trees down, and then to begin fighting the army.

But the army did not stop, and the Mormons returned home. Had a battle resulted it would surely have been a bloody one. The Mormons had among them many hard-riding, straight-shooting men who had learned everything there was to know about their mountains, and who certainly were not afraid to fight.

But the Echo Canyon War, or Mormon War, started, ran its course, and ended, without a man on either side being killed as a direct result of fighting.

15. What The Mormons Did

HISTORY IS NO MORE THAN THE WRITTEN record of what people said and did. But just suppose that the Mormons had never said or done anything.

Doubtless, even if the Mormons had not gone

there, the Salt Lake Valley would have been settled. Sooner or later someone would have seen the rich possibilities of the country and he would have pointed them out to others. But how long would it have taken?

However, rather than wonder about what might have happened had the Mormons not gone west, it is possible to point out part of what happened because they did go. Their accomplishments are many—far too many to list in full.

It seems to this writer that one of the most important contributions the Mormons made to their country was the example they set.

When they left Nauvoo they had only what they could load into their carts and wagons. They were in desperate need of almost everything, and they thought that, if they built roads and blockhouses, the United States would pay them money which they needed badly. But the country they intended to enter was prized so little, and the Mormons themselves were held

in such small regard, that the Government refused to consider their offer or to pay them
anything at all.

The Mormons might have quit then. They
might have stopped where they were, assured
each other that they could not possibly go on
unless they got some help, and done nothing.
But they didn't.

Getting money where they could, supplying
their own labor, they built the roads and forts
anyhow.

What must be done, they did. There were no
anxious agricultural advisers standing at their
shoulders when they sank their plow points into
the desert; they could find out how to grow
crops in such a land or they could starve. The
first transcontinental railway went through Ogden, Utah, and by-passed Salt Lake City. It was
the Mormons themselves who built additional
railroads in their state. They built highways,
bridges, telegraph and telephone lines, factories.

This independence of spirit and thought is

still very much a trait of the Mormons. They know what they want, and they neither ask nor expect anyone except themselves to get it for them.

The Mormons were unbelievably industrious colonizers. From 1847, when they founded Salt Lake City, until 1877, when Brigham Young died, they themselves established three hundred and sixty colonies. Some of these were hundreds of miles from Salt Lake City. The farthest was San Bernardino, in southern California, more than 750 miles away.

It is very doubtful if there are more than a handful of cities and towns in our Mountain and Pacific Coast states which the Mormons did not help settle or whose settlement they did not influence directly. The Mormon settlements brought civilization to a vast wilderness. People from the Northwest, Washington and Oregon, Canada, and even Mexico, came to the Mormons for seeds, draft animals, cattle, and help without which settlement of their own areas would have been much more difficult.

Though the Mormons had their Indian wars, it was always their desire to live at peace with the Indians. They were very successful, and many a wagon train got through without Indian trouble because it had a Mormon guide. The Mormons did much to make the trails safe for those who came after them.

The Mormons did at least as much as anyone else to open the West to those from other countries. In Brigham Young's lifetime alone the Mormon settlements grew from 20,000 to 150,000 people, many of whom were born outside the United States. They brought with them skills and talents which have contributed vastly to the development and progress of the entire country.

Beyond any doubt, the Mormons were the first to develop any worth-while irrigation systems in America. They mastered the science of bringing water to dry land, and of making that land productive. They contributed much to the art of dry farming, or farming without any water except that already in the land. Because of irrigation and dry farming, millions of acres of what would have been worthless land now grows some of our finest crops.

Long before anyone else even considered such a thing seriously, Mormon women had the right to vote. They were at all times the equals of their men and they had a full voice in community affairs.

There is almost no craft or industry which the Mormons did not encourage. And they backed the fine arts just as enthusiastically. One of the first buildings they constructed in Salt Lake City was a theater. Brigham Young himself took under his personal care people of special talents such as artists, sculptors, architects, poets, and musicians. The Mormons did everything possible to encourage the establishment of schools, colleges, and universities.

The list does not end here, nor will it ever end. Today Mormons are highly respected citizens of every state in the Union and their missionaries are in almost every foreign country. They still adhere to the principles that inspired Joseph Smith and Brigham Young and, true to the word of these men, they are a happy and prosperous people. The list of their achievements can have no ending because every year Mormons, who are found in every constructive activity, add to it.

Though they are now world-wide, their capital is still Salt Lake City. Anybody who visits there will not be able to tell a Mormon from a non-Mormon by his dress, his speech, or his manner. But anyone who stops in Salt Lake City, and who will use his eyes to see and his ears to hear, will discover for himself that the Mormons today are not greatly different from those of Brigham Young's day. The traveler will be sure of a warm and courteous welcome.

And he will come away, as we did, with the thought that he has been among a fine and wonderful people.

Index

Allen, James, 55-56
Angel Moroni, 5

Bear River, 82; *map*, 91
Big Elk (chief), 58-59
Big Mountain, 93
Boggs, L. W., 7, 76, 79
Book of Mormon, 5
Bordeaux, James, 76
Boston, Massachusetts, 17
Brannon, Samuel, 83-88, 107-08
Bridger, Jim, 81-82, 165
Bridger (fort), 89, 165; *map*, 71
Brockmann (man), 61
Brooklyn (ship), 83, 85
Brown, James, 108, 140
Brown, Samuel, 140
Buchanan, President, 169
Bullock, Thomas, 69, 104

California, 52, 56, 77, 85-86, 88, 108, 116-17, 146; gold rush, 156-61
Carthage, Illinois, 14
Catholic missionaries, 132
Chicago, Illinois, 7; *map,* 54
Children, 112, 135
City Creek, 95, 104, 144
Clayton, William, 69-70, 75, 84, 137
Clifford, Major, 60
Council Bluffs, Iowa, 53, 133-34
Crickets, 123-29, 138
Cummings, Governor, 168

Deaths, 120
Deseret (state), 116, 141, 162; *map,* 115
Deseret News, 161
Donner Party, 90-92

179